DATE DUE

MAY 27 2003

GAYLORD

PRINTED IN U.S.A.

To build a
CIVILIZATION
of Love
Catholic Education
and Service Learning

© 2001
National Catholic Educational Association
1077 30th Street, NW, Suite 100
Washington, DC 20007-3852
ISBN 1-55833-261-8

Dedication

To Pauline,
Your fidelity to Christ and your delight in the Spirit's roaring
presence in me has brought God to many people.
And so each day I whisper...Thank You God, for the gift of
Pauline.

Contents

Foreword

During the writing of this book, a former student of mine, Jessica Conzo, who had just returned from a semester in Costa Rica, visited me. For her junior year abroad, she chose a program of service that brought her into the Costa Rican reality. Her testimony below shows how service learning experiences impacted her during her high school days. In preface to all that will be said about the value of service learning, I offer her witness as the best reason for considering service learning as an integral aspect of Catholic education:

Just after my seventeenth birthday, I made a long awaited trip to Haiti as part of a school group known as the Haiti Club. Our objectives were to provide resources to our "sister school" in Haiti and to educate ourselves and those in our community about conditions in Haiti. This group acted as a vehicle through which others could contribute to help those in need. This trip had been postponed previously two or three times, presenting us with our first experience of the uncertainty of things that Haitians encounter every day.

Haiti was like nothing that I imagined. Even today, it is something that I remember with awe. The smells, the people, their smiles…everything comes back to me. It is never far from me. To write a check or to send supplies is great, but it leaves you in the same state of mind as before you wrote the numbers or went shopping. To travel so close to our own country and yet so far away in other ways, to hear the vendors' calls on the streets, to smell the earth, the food, the people, and to see the way of life of another country and culture is irreplaceable.

In a country where 20% of the children die of diarrhea before their fifth birthday, where 500,000 children live in domestic servitude, and where 85% of the people cannot read or write, the strength, the love, the hope, and the faith of the people is overwhelming. A famous Haitian proverb says, "Tankou wozo nou pliye, men nou pa kase," which translates to "Like reeds we bend, but do not break." This is the strength of Haiti.

Haiti is the poorest country in the Western hemisphere, yet, the people are always willing to give their neighbors all that they can spare. The country is rich with love, rich in the spirit of God. In Eyes of the Heart, *President Jean Bertrand Aristide writes, "We begin with what we see in front of us. I cannot see God, but I can see you. I cannot see God, but I see the child in front of the woman, the man, and me. Through them, through this material world in which we live, we know God. Through them, we know and we experience love; we glimpse and seek justice."[1]*

There have been many times when I have questioned God and religion. I have wondered where my faith would take me. In Haiti, I found answers, and I saw so clearly all the opportunities and freedoms that I have. I realized that I was given these opportunities to use them. My experiences in Haiti left me with an understanding of who I am, of what my purpose is. Haiti filled me with a passion to share in others' lives, to learn about other cultures, and to actively create opportunities for others.

Discipleship is different from volunteer work in that discipleship involves participation with a unique spirit that volunteer work lacks. This spirit is shared with all those that are touched by the work, and a circle is created where the Spirit flows among all who participate. Volunteer work accomplishes many wonderful things, but if people close themselves off from accepting the Spirit, then they break the circle. Volunteering out of duty instead of desire breaks the circle.

Where does the desire come from? Those that touched my life in Haiti were overflowing with this energy. They allowed me into their lives and gave me the opportunity to understand the importance of the work that I was doing. Young people have very open minds and hearts. Time has not crammed them with cynicism or hatred. Children crave knowledge and are receptive to the Spirit. The younger the children are when they receive this energy, the stronger it will become in them and the more people it will benefit.

Haiti will always hold a spot deep in my heart. Haiti was my awakening to the reality of the number of people throughout the world that are in need.

Jessica Conzo
Worcester, MA
January 1, 2001   Feast of the Solemnity of Mary

Acknowledgements

I have come to realize that although writers are compelled to write, many ideas and experiences that go into a final manuscript are simply beyond the writer's immediate milieu. So much of who we are is the result of a life shared with others, and the writer can easily forget people who deserve acknowledgement. My relationship with the Beloved and my journey with the poor and oppressed have not been without the loving support and wisdom of so many good people. I live in gratitude to countless disciples who have nourished my faith. What is shared in these pages is undoubtedly the fruit of many such relationships.

God has energized me most clearly through my students. I gratefully acknowledge their wisdom, vitality, passion for justice, and love of God, as they have inspired and influenced mine. I have worked alongside many saints in them. Their efforts in building a civilization of love continually give me courage.

I am grateful to NCEA, and in particular Sr. Mary Frances Taymans, SND, Ed.D., Molly Dunn, and Brian Vaccaro for their commitment in editing and publishing this manuscript and for their patience in making it happen. Those who have carefully read through drafts include: Rev. T. Becket A. Franks, OSB; Pauline Lajoie; Frank George; Kallin Johnson; Sr. Teresa Fallon, SND; and Steven A. Pinkston. They have my sincere gratitude.

Introduction

In his World Youth Day message of November 1995, Pope John Paul II encouraged people to "...oppose what today seems to be the 'disintegration of civilization' in order vigorously to reaffirm the 'civilization of love,' which alone can bring true peace and justice."[2] This book assists teachers, youth ministers, service coordinators, and administrators who help young people take up the cause of building a civilization of love by performing works of peace and justice through service learning rooted in Catholic social teaching.

Catholic education is distinctive in its formation of disciples. While Catholic education offers service learning that promotes effective citizenship and character development, thus satisfying the objectives of secular institutions, it also extends beyond such goals to the formation of disciples with a lifetime calling to a servanthood that builds the reign of God. Be it in the school, parish, or youth ministry program, Catholic educators and ministers play an essential role in developing the disciples of the future.

Jesus is calling young people today, surely as he called his first band of disciples. It is in service learning experiences, rooted firmly in the Gospel and lived in the Spirit, that many young people meet Jesus. They meet him in the marginalized and the suffering, those whose rights have been denied and whose hopes have been betrayed. It is in learning to love as Jesus loved and to love those whom Jesus loved that young people move from simple volunteer service to the miracle of ministry.

The first four chapters of this book offer theoretical considerations regarding the essential elements of Catholic service learning: the theology of ministry, notable adolescent milestones, Catholic social teaching, and curriculum development. The final chapters are more practical, offering operative insight into the challenges associated with taking education beyond the classroom walls and retaining the ministerial dimensions. Known variously as service, character education, and ministry, what is discussed herein as "service learning" refers to projects and programs that prepare teenagers and young adults for their ministry as Jesus' disciples.

Genuine Catholic service programs exude John Paul II's clear and unmistakable call to the young: "In this world you are called to live fraternally, not as a utopia but as a real possibility; in this society, you are called as true missionaries of Christ to build the civilization of love."[3]

It is my great hope that the theological reflections and practical suggestions offered here enliven your ministry, nourishing the desire of young people to follow Christ and serve the world as He did.

To Build a
Civilization
of Love

Catholic Education
and Service Learning

Chapter 1

A Theology of Mission and Ministry for the Young

Ministry and Miracles

Several years ago while ministering in Port-Au-Prince, Haiti, my friends and I wandered into a hidden room in the local hospital. Herein, we discovered Haiti's throw-away children lying still and mute in cage-like cribs. A single glance laid bare the rejected children, starving for food and affection. They ranged in age from infancy to ten years old, and they were alone, dirty, and wearing stained, filthy rags on a small portion of their bodies. They were rigid from lack of movement and their sounds were animal-like from a lack of communication. Large rats waited in prey in the corners of the room. Never had I known a more pitiable place.

One small baby moved us each to tears. Her name was Immaculata, and she was hydrocephalic. Her large head seemed five times greater than her petite frame, which was only a little more than bones. One could, however, detect a hint of a smile from the corner of her mouth, the only sign of hope in this devastating scene. I wept over Immaculata, much as I imagined Jesus wept over Jerusalem. As I begged God to have mercy on Immaculata, I imagined that if she lived in my city, adequate medical care would afford her both comfort and progress. Left here in this room, she would undoubtedly die. I prayed in utter desperation — "Please, please dear God, have mercy on this child."

Years later, my godson Kyle was killed by an aggressive driver. He lived for eleven days and, during that time, was cared for with incredible precision in the pediatric intensive care unit at a prominent hospital. Kyle fought hard for his life as medical personnel assisted him with every grace and technology known to humankind. Committed to honoring his memory and the heroic efforts of these doctors and nurses, Kyle's mom and I delivered a large teddy bear to every child in the unit that Christmas. As we walked the halls, the coordinating nurse told us about a Haitian child in the unit whose name was "Immaculata." I responded that I had once worked with a baby named Immaculata in Haiti, but that her situation was truly a hopeless one.

As we entered the very last room, a cheerful woman greeted us, calling me by name. She was obviously the child's mother. Although I didn't know her, she had recognized me from the publicity surrounding my work in Haiti. I looked into the bed and there was the unmistakable smile of baby Immaculata, now five years old. I was stunned into silence and awe. Here was Immaculata before my very eyes, in a hospital with all the love, affection, and medical expertise I had begged God for so many years ago. A family that had seen the pictures from Haiti made a trip to find Immaculata. They had adopted her and were living a mere 20 minutes from my home.

God answers our deepest desires in the most miraculous ways. The compassionate One works wonders with the hopes of children like Immaculata, with her adoptive parents, with medical personnel, and yes, with my own desires. That Christmas, when John's Gospel declared how God so loved the world that He sent His only

Son, grace was born in me again. How very good the good God is to have given me treasures stored in darkness. Are there miracles? Yes, there are.

I begin with this story because it confirms that each and every act people perform in service to God brings about the reign "as it is in heaven." Ministry and service involve miracles everyday. God is deeply involved with human life. Introducing young people to the world of service learning is more than helping them to organize the good they do, or make the positive social changes that are needed. Community service learning is first and foremost awakening them to the presence and miracles of God.

Not all service has as dramatic an outcome as Immaculata's story. For the most part, people never see the fruits of their labors, but their efforts in the "vineyard" do provide the underlying hope by which the world lives each day. Supporting young people in the ministry of service learning initiates them into the world of God's mysterious ways. It moves them deeply into mission and discipleship and awakens the eyes of their hearts to the mighty works of God and the salvation of God's people, activities in which they are principle actors.

Service Learning is Ministry and Mission

The inherent difference between service learning in Catholic educational settings and the service experiences mandated by the courts, assigned by the public school, or offered by secular organizations is in the expressed motive and intended outcome. The sole purpose of Christian ministry is to bring about the reign of God, and the intended outcome is complete and unconditional love. This kingdom is realized with the elimination of all that is unjust, by embracing the marginalized as brothers and sisters. It is affected by accepting the call to be like Christ.

This is not to say that the grace of God is not active in endeavors lacking a specific religious character or intent, but that educational programs with a Christian focus intentionally work in unison with the grace of God. Christian service learning has a distinct mandate to accomplish this aim, and there can be no compromising this mandate, for herein Christian meaning is found and celebrated. Indeed, it is for its practice of the corporal and spiritual works of mercy that the young can identify with and respect the

Church. Matthew gives a very clear picture of the final judgment in his twenty-fifth chapter: The division will occur between those who built the civilization of love from those who did not—those who fed the hungry, gave drink to the thirsty, clothed the naked, visited the imprisoned and sick, sheltered the homeless, and buried the dead. Christians can take enormous pride in a worldwide ministry—service learning accomplished as ministry initiates the next generation into this greatness.

Baptism and Service Learning

The primary task, then, is to propel students towards a theology of mission. Catholic identity starts with the gift of Baptism. To be one with the Father and secured by the Spirit in love and truth provides individuals with the sanctity needed to make God's presence in the world visible to others. It is through a re-identification as daughters and sons of God that people are made ministers of the kingdom. Such is the baptismal heritage, our origin of both identity and call. Christian ministry then involves any action accomplished in the name of the Father, in union with Jesus, and consummated by the Spirit. The baptized perform the human action needed to restore life and give love as righteously graced members of the family of God. Catholic educators promote service learning as ministerial when it is accomplished in unison with the grace of God. Thus, animating students with a theological focus for service learning begins by awakening baptismal grace.

The theology of Baptism emphasizes questions young people often ask. From pre-school to high school, young people want to know: Who am I? What makes me special? For what purpose did God make me? What did God give me that is unique and different from others? By revitalizing the gift of human worth and dignity, which God has bestowed on each person, ministers of service education create the basis for understanding a theology of mission. The very taproot of work and prayer is kinship with the Creator, brotherhood with Jesus, and reliance on the Spirit. Beginning to answer the essential questions of self with a baptismal theology, young people come to experience the relational grace of God in their own lives. It is this power that informs and forms service as ministry. Helping young people employ the grace of baptism prepares them for Christian ministry.

A Theological Foundation For Young Servants

In his work, *Theology of Ministry*, Rev. Thomas Franklin O'Meara, OP explores the nature of Christian ministry. Applying sound theological principles to service learning objectives lays the foundation for nurturing ministers, not simply volunteers. Fr. O'Meara believes that "Christian ministry is the public activity of a baptized follower of Jesus Christ, flowing from the Spirit's charism and an individual personality on behalf of a Christian community to witness, to serve, and to realize the kingdom of God."[4]

There is something potent about public activity. Its public witness makes a commitment more powerful. In opening oneself to the criticisms and affections of others, by making an action public, people testify to what is in their hearts. Christians' motives can be questioned and their ideas criticized. While there is much to be said for humility, the public witness of a story such as Immaculata's nourishes the seeds of hope in the hearer and gives glory to God, whose mysterious ways accomplish these miracles. Thus, it is fundamental to train young people in the value of public activity and witness.

Young people need to experience how an action becomes a dividend for the whole community when done in the name of Jesus. It is owned and celebrated by all. All are energized by the good that it accomplishes. Jesus assured His followers that His work would continue through the Spirit. Young people struggling to know the difference between secular service and ministerial activity need to encounter the gift of the Spirit within themselves. They need to know and celebrate their ministerial action as public activity that flows from the Spirit's charism in their individual personalities. Finally, they need to realize that they act on behalf of something bigger than themselves: the Christian community. Young people desire to be vested in something greater than themselves; they too want to realize the Kingdom as much as the great saints did.

Confirmation and Service Learning

Preparing for the Sacrament of Confirmation is a meaningful time for young people as they come alive with the Holy Spirit's gifts. As such, it is the perfect time to help them understand the nature of the Holy Spirit's action in their personal stories. As they choose saints they wish to emulate, it is a wonderful time to bestow on them the heritage of loving kindness found in the lives of the saints whose ministries were marked with a profound sense of God. It is important that the communion of saints be grasped by young Catholics as a viable connection to service ministry.

Having nurtured the Christian mandate to ministry through the early years, adolescents will be accustomed to service learning as a public and communal activity intended to build a civilization of love. This requires a recurring awareness and reflection of service as a gift of grace from God. Service experiences that are understood as such help each young person become more of a minister and less of a volunteer.

Confronting the Antithesis of the Kingdom

A theology of mission that inspires young people requires a clear focus on the ministry of Jesus. Fr. O'Meara notes that: "Jesus' ministry is not only a ministry of preaching the kingdom, but one of confronting the antitheses of the kingdom. These are evil, sin, madness, want, injustice, and death; they are the visible effect in our human condition of fallenness or sin." [5]

Given the state of affairs locally, nationally, and internationally, one could easily give in to despair. Add in the negative influence of the media and music, and it is amazing that young people have any faith at all. Yet, they do. Instantaneous communication has resulted in a generation with a fairly accurate sense of the world's affairs. Young people are not naive about evil and sin. Their daily lives are oftentimes surrounded by madness and injustice. They need to realize that Jesus did not shy away from the things that were uncomfortable, painful, or scary. They must be encouraged not only to confront societal issues but also assisted in facing the challenges of their immediate surroundings: violence, racism, sex for sport, and drugs.

Indeed, at the dawn of a new millennium, it is amazing how similar our time is to that of Jesus. Young people today have the advantage, or perhaps disadvantage, of seeing the problems of the world in an instant. The visible effect on the human condition that Fr. O'Meara refers to has no less an impact on young people. There are many strong young people whose fears for the human family are deep. How fortunate teachers of the Word are that Jesus' boldness in confronting evil is so apparent in the Gospel! What credibility Christ already has with young readers as they behold Him "confronting the antitheses of the kingdom." Young people naturally thirst for justice, and it is not difficult to convince them of the need to do more than simply talk about the problems of the world.

Jesus: A Unique Minister, A Unique Ministry

Another important theological element for service learning or mission training about which Fr. O'Meara speaks helps to focus on the uniqueness of Jesus' ministry. He contends, "Jesus' ministry became striking in His inclusion of the poor, the marginalized, and the oppressed. He called people to a discipleship that was more than the temple priesthood, more than a rabbinic internship. By calling a variety of men and women and by forcefully explaining the reign of God, Jesus showed that others are to carry on His ministry."[6]

When forming service programs, Christians are challenged to go beyond the safe or simple projects, to the messy, even frightful places, in order to get at the root of society's problems. In conflict with systems and outdated rules, Jesus maintained contact with those who could change systems as well as those whom the systems oppressed. This challenge remains. In order to retain the ministerial spirit of Jesus, young people must be led to places where they may be uncomfortable. In addressing social change, service can take place at a diocesan meeting, a news conference, or an inner city soup kitchen—places young people usually are not found. Admittedly difficult, this challenge is at the root of all Catholic social teaching and thus is an essential element in Catholic service programs.

Fr. O'Meara emphasizes that the call of Jesus does not take place in comfort. Thus, service cannot merely act as a nice entry on a résumé or college entrance application. Jesus dared to establish a service ministry that could potentially bring young people to places that might not impress college admission directors. Fr. O'Meara also offers an interesting insight that Jesus called a variety of people to explain the reign of God, and He did not compromise the message. Jesus had followers from all walks of life; this counsels all people to value each and every young person as a vessel of God and each opportunity as one to openly proclaim the righteousness of God and the coming of the kingdom.

Awakening young people to their inclusion in God's kingdom empowers them to give witness with the full strength of God's grace. Although practicalities do exist, it is important to note that obstacles do not take Jesus's followers too far beyond Fr. O'Meara's illumination. Simply stated, the mission and ministry of Jesus must shape the mission and ministry of service learning in Catholic educational settings.

Young People Confirm Fr. O'Meara's Theology

Many young people have baptismal-graced experiences of service driven by the Holy Spirit. They enliven others through their continued work with the Spirit. Their commitment demonstrates that a love of service coexists with a service of love. Both young and old disciples share the hallmark of a baptized Christian: unconditional and sacrificial love. The Christian educator ensures that service experiences for the young are not devoid of love. In this way, one truly teaches the Christian way of life.

For several years, I have taught a *Peace through Justice* program to seniors that structures the learning around a shared service project. The course requires the students to perform the following tasks:

- Assess community needs.
- Adopt one need as the focus of the course study.
- Develop a solution by designing a program to fit the need.
- Write a grant proposal to obtain funding for the program.
- Fully implement and evaluate the program.
- Make plans for the program's continuance after graduation.

The course length is one academic school year. Since this course is required of all seniors, typically 80 students are challenged to work out this single task together. A particularly gratifying year occurred when students assessing the community's need discovered a complete lack of Alcoholics Anonymous meetings in the city that provided childcare. Thus, these students concluded that it would be difficult for alcoholic parents to participate in this self-help group. Imagine the impact they had once they collaborated with a shelter for alcoholic, homeless women to co-sponsor an AA meeting with childcare services. Their insight, unconditional love, and ability to work together provided an important service in the city. Their very successful program met Fr. O'Meara's conditions that ministry must take the form of public activity, confront injustice, deal with visible effects of fallenness, and include the poor, the marginalized, and the oppressed.

On another occasion, I received a call from a psychiatric facility for teenagers that was seeking help with a prom for the young people in its program. I still recall vividly the enthusiasm and generosity of my students who wanted nothing more than to help. As they planned and strategized, it was clear that the generosity of Christ had entered their hearts. One could clearly see the Christ who did not give up, whose overwhelming, passionate love reached out to the poor time and again. As these young students reached out to the "poor in Spirit" without fear, Christ was powerfully present.

The students not only convinced local dress shops and tuxedo stores to donate new clothing, they created a store-like setting so that the young people could come, shop, and try on outfits. They not only provided makeup and hair ornaments, they went to the psychiatric facility to help their newfound friends get ready for the big night. The students engaged the free services of a disc jockey, decorated the hall, baked desserts, and make favors. There was plenty to be done, and in sharing the many tasks, they developed an authentic Christian community.

These students realized they were about God's business, and for them it was an encounter with the Kingdom. Being rooted in the Gospel mission to the poor, they understood the heart of Jesus as well as their own hearts. They were in a facility that was unlike anything they had ever experienced. Yet, they found a way to be comfortable. Most importantly, they put Jesus' intent into practice and clearly accepted the call to discipleship with the marginalized. Their achievement was seen and felt in their obvious joy, another hallmark of those who do things simply for the Glory of God.

To Go Where Jesus Went

The obligation to serve where Christ dictates is one of the most challenging requests but clearly a crucial concern in developing a theology of mission and ministry with young people. Our diocese sponsors an evening each month for those infected and affected by AIDS. The program includes shared prayer, dinner, and a social gathering. For a number of years, my sophomore morality class has worked with the Diocesan AIDS Ministry Office to prepare the evening. Working with a population very different from themselves, students willingly accept the formidable task of designing prayers for a group wounded and sometimes lacking in hope. Realizing that Jesus, in service to God, stood not with the wealthy and powerful, but with the poor and needy, is a powerful theological lesson for young people. That Jesus was so energetic in his inclusion of the least of the Kingdom of God is a key message for the young to learn. Adopting an option for the poor is close to many young people, who themselves may have been or continue to be outsiders. Be it the strong cliques common in schools or the frequent demeaning treatment they receive at first jobs, it is not a far reach for many young people to understand oppression.

> Paradoxically, in identifying with Christ, vulnerable and wounded, people come to know the Resurrection. Experiencing vulnerability helps young people understand the nature of the cross and the Resurrection, the absolute core of the Christian faith.

Ministry, Vulnerability, and Loving the Poor

Jesus preached justice that was familial. God's passion for justice is sanctioned in Jesus' vulnerability as He lived the life of a scorned servant. "Let the same mind be in you that was in Christ Jesus, who though He was equal to God, He did not regard equality with God something to be exploited, but emptied Himself, taking the nature of a slave, being born in human likeness" (Phil. 2:5-7). It was not enough for Jesus to affect change in a system; He personally gave His will and freedom. Christians are asked to do the same.

People experience the salvific nature of God in loving the poor and becoming one with them. Paradoxically, in identifying with Christ, vulnerable and wounded, people come to know the Resurrection. Experiencing vulnerability helps young people understand the nature of the cross and the Resurrection, the absolute core of the Christian faith. Challenging though the transfer is, most young people feel vulnerability every day; thus, the Resurrection is actually Good News to them on a personal level.

Standing in solidarity with the poor brings about a strong desire to change the system that perpetuates injustice and vulnerability. The young will need an introduction to the underlying problems that plague the poor. What to them may seem like personal incapability may indeed be systemic weakness or a sinful social structure. Frequently, a great leap needs to be taken to become a minister of love; it requires that people stop blaming the victim and look at the system.

> Ministry to the poor and marginalized confronts not only the antithesis of the Kingdom, but makes people confront their own fears as well.

In yet another experience of my *Peace through Justice* class, I saw my students meet an actual need. The nearby public schools had lost their funding for arts programming, and my students decided to help reintroduce the arts back into the curriculum in an elementary school in the poorest section of the city. When the students visited the school, they were alarmed to witness children in the third grade smoking cigarettes. Immediately, the class saw the additional need for anti-smoking and drug education that could be linked with the arts.

Working collaboratively and with zest typical of youth, some seventy-six students created skits, songs, dance routines, and visual art projects that involved the entire elementary school. The curriculum culminated with an evening of entertainment for the parents of both groups of students. The visual and performing arts were reintroduced in the curriculum, the young students thoroughly had investigated the devastation of alcohol, drugs, and smoking, and the *Peace through Justice* course began to understand the real work of service ministry. Through planning and carrying out their lessons, they came to experience the vulnerability of the poor. They also came to understand the cycle of poverty, and subsequently to give up their biases towards the poor.

What this has to do with developing a theology of mission and ministry will be examined in greater depth later on, but for now it is important to realize that the students chose to act as Jesus would have acted. The follower of Christ is called to minister where the antithesis of the kingdom lies. "Fear not," is a phrase often repeated by Jesus. Ministry to the poor and marginalized confronts not only the antithesis of the Kingdom, but makes people confront their own fears as well.

No more have I known Christ than in those students who have worked with the poorest of the poor. Students working in places such as Haiti or Kenya have not only had their eyes opened, but their hearts have been enlightened as well. Young people who have experienced places like the hospital where we found Immaculata have come to know the power of miracles within their ministry to the physically poor.

On one trip to Haiti, my students and I worked in a government-operated nursing home that had not received attention in years. Entering the patients' rooms, we saw unbelievable filth. The flea-infested dwellings were small, dank, and dark. Patients' water containers—merely discarded beer bottles—were dirty with dead cockroaches in them. A most pitiable place, the adults on the trip would not stay in the rooms because of the squalor, stench, and infestations. The young students, however, brave and moved with compassion, declared that they simply could not leave those rooms in that condition. They set their hands and hearts about cleaning and scrubbing. Amazed at their ingenuity, I watched in awe as they cleaned the rooms, bleached out the bottles, and made stoppers to keep the water in the bottles clean. While it seemed like a small change for humankind, I knew that day that these young people had found and invested themselves in the reign of God.

Young people are hungry for a theological meaning of their experiences. Applying the principles of theology and ministry to the planning and designing of Catholic educational service projects and programs can help give young people the meaning they are seeking. In continuing the discussion of the specifics of making service programs worthwhile experiences of the kingdom, do not forget these basic principles for developing ministers and disciples for the kingdom of God: ministry is public and flows from a sacramental relationship with the trinity; ministry is singularly connected to the reign of God; ministry confronts the madness, evil, and fallenness of the world; and ministry is a relationship with the poor and marginalized. Take joy in remembering how often it actually happens.

Chapter 2

Called to the Vineyard: Service Learning for the Developing Youth

The Vineyard Needs Tending

The United States is one of the most powerful countries in the world, with technological advances and educational benefits far exceeding most countries. Still, every day in this wealthy nation children die from abuse, violence, and poverty. Many women have late or no prenatal care, and teenagers become parents at earlier ages. Young people drop out of school, are imprisoned in adult jails, are homeless, and are misused for sex in a variety of forums. Many men, women, and children are poor; many elderly struggle to make ends meet. Overcrowded emergency shelters in cities turn people away, and more people than ever can expect to experience homelessness. This translates into wounded communities of empty, directionless children and adults living the "fallenness of the human condition." The daily headlines confirm that this struggle involves every community in the United States.

The international situation fares no better. The Hunger Project of the United Nations estimates that about 24,000 people die every day from hunger or hunger related diseases.[7] CARE reports that ten percent of children in developing countries die before the age of five.[8] Using these statistics, the young people in my morality class recently calculated that 6,417 people die of hunger during the course of one school day; 4,812 of them are children. Over the course of an academic year, just for the hours we are in session, a total of 794,062 children die. According to the Institute for Food and Development, "besides death, chronic malnutrition also causes impaired vision, listlessness, stunted growth, and greatly increased susceptibility to disease."[9]

In *The Gospel of Life*, Pope John Paul II alleges that we are living in a culture of death. Such a civilization disrespects life in all its stages and conditions. Urging a change in our fundamental attitude, the Pope promotes a radical movement towards the protection of life. Both national and international conditions support the need for such a basic change. The development of service programs that foster disciples of life is a good first step in this direction.

The Formative Power of Service Learning

Service learning with its formative possibilities and healing capacities is a vital part of Catholic education. Serving others meets the needs of both the individual and the community. There is a natural symmetry between a young person's developmental needs, their limitless passion for truth and justice, and the Church's clear mandate to address social justice issues. Helping young people effectively define and use their virtues for the good of the community is one of the most formidable ministerial tasks of Catholic educators. It can also be one of the most enjoyable. Along with infancy, teenagers undergo a dramatic peak in human growth. These years, rapid with social, moral, cognitive, and identity development, go so quickly that many teenagers admit they can hardly keep up with understanding themselves. The early and later teenage years have significantly different milestones; thus, they shall be examined separately.

The Younger Adolescent and the Significance of Service Learning

Service experiences are quite advantageous for the younger adolescent, aged eleven to fifteen, whose developmental needs are undeniably suited to experiential learning. Although single service events more readily captivate them, an ongoing service commitment can also be considered. The younger teenager's need to belong socially and to develop relationships with a variety of people is nurtured through experiences with a diverse population. Experimenting with a variety of behaviors and relationships is necessary for the maturation of strong social skills. Service learning can assist young teenagers in developing a context for moral duty, permitting their inner convictions to be put into practice and ultimately to be solidly held. The strong desire to be needed and to belong works to their advantage. In addition, young teenagers often have more free time than older adolescents because their interests are not yet strongly developed, and they do not yet have driver's licenses or hold jobs.

Young teenagers are bustling with cognitive growth. Their ability to think abstractly is heightening. Approaching formal operational thinking, they move progressively from the concrete of black and white thinking to the inevitability of gray matters. The reflective process inherent in skillful service learning helps them learn to appreciate issues with a myriad of possibilities. The practicality of having a situation with which to consider alternatives and complexities helps progress the process of abstract thinking. This can be a slow process, and most young people need some assistance in this area.

Service learning likewise helps the young teenager's developing sense of identity. Desperately desiring to belong and setting aside childlike behaviors, teenagers search for heroes, significant adults, and a group membership that feels safe. With these securities, they can become comfortable asking life's meaningful questions: Who am I? Who am I becoming? What am I? What do I want to be? Service learning allows these fragile identity-seekers to experience independence and individual choices that reinforce a developing sense of autonomy. Yet, it offers the comfort of not being solely responsible for things beyond their capability.

Single-event service opportunities sponsored by educators with expertise are wonderful for the younger teenager. Younger teenagers can be overwhelmed with finding, selecting, or creating a service experience. Not being committed to a single setting, but experiencing a variety of groups and endeavors, supports the younger person in identifying his or her interests and skills. This does not necessarily mean continually establishing a new group. The ongoing parish or school youth group can provide a variety of single service experiences in which the young person has the security of the group with the benefit of a variety of situations.

Most importantly, participating in outreach steeped in Gospel values enhances the faith development of the young teenager. In helping to shape young people rooted in the Christian tradition, adults must assist them in deepening their personal relationship with God and establishing active participation in the reign of God. Young people are anxious to "talk the talk" and "walk the walk"; they are seeking a personal faith identity. They are ready to hear anew the Christian story and recognize how they can become a living part of it. They are no longer satisfied to simply know that Jesus loved, but can now hear the call to live Jesus' love. Helping young teenagers to establish a means of belonging in the Christian community, to enact their developing identity, and to use their skills for building a civilization of love is an arduous but joy-filled challenge for Catholic education.

The Older Adolescent and the Significance of Service

Older teenagers, aged sixteen to nineteen, have their own set of maturation needs. Developmental milestones in the social, cognitive, identity, moral, and faith areas are significantly different from those of younger teenagers. Even more so, then, is the need for effective service experiences. The central labor of the older adolescent is in the area of identity development. The question "Who I am" is rooted in powerful new experiences such as acquiring a driver's license, maintaining the responsibilities of a first job, choosing a college or post high school experience, and articulating a philosophy of life. Service experiences help the individual to solidify the Christian-based view of life. Regularly performed service, perhaps one to two hours a week for at least a year, offers the young person a chance to conceptualize their Christian self. As older teenagers confront issues of career and lifestyle, an ongoing commitment to a single site can be helpful. While single-event experiences are helpful for younger teenagers, living through the struggles of an ongoing commitment to a single site is necessary for the older teenager.

Cognitively, the older adolescent has an expanded capacity in abstract thinking. Thus, the reflective element of service learning is now intrinsic in addressing life's important questions and perceiving its central meaning. Older teenagers can come to realize the value of unconditional love. Now able to question why, they can conceptualize problems, institutions, and systems that create and sustain the oppression of people. The ability to view a more complicated world gives them an opportunity to experience the need for a deeper level of commitment and skill.

Older adolescents approach moral matters with a greater degree of reasoning, allowing them to bring greater awareness to their service experience. The ability to critique social values and recognize moral imperatives changes the service experience from "doing good to feel good," to a response of moral necessity. Universal principles can be more easily considered as the young adult will now internalize a moral value system. Justice and love as components of service now go beyond "what I am supposed to do" as the teenager can comprehend the interrelationship of these essential elements. For this reason, it is essential to fortify them with Catholic social teaching.

For the older teenager, faith development is marked by taking responsibility for one's own spirituality. Service to the Church itself through liturgical roles, religious education, and direct assistance to the poor can deepen their connection to the community's faith story. Relationships with adults who are alive in the faith can now be mutual. A fruitful experience of service including reflection and prayer with a mentor can meet their need to experience deep relational faith. Many older adolescents identify themselves as "spiritual," but not "religious." They desire a deep, interpersonal relationship with God and the Church, moving beyond the mere practice of institutional religion. The desire to form a deep consciousness of both faith and service is acute in many older adolescents. The prayer life of the older teen is slowly moving from the ego-centered, "I want to pass my algebra test," to the needs of those whom they have met and loved in service.

Service can be equally satisfying for young people and for those they serve. It is clear that there is much to be done in this hungry, hurting world. Luckily, God provides much through the natural tendencies of the young person to accomplish it.

Guiding the Teenager in God's Kingdom

Christians are called to build the reign of God locally, nationally, and globally. Service learning programs should be structured with the realization that God invites young people to minister in each of these realms. The frequently heard criticism that the United States should not be spending its resources, time, or energy in other parts of the world when so many of its own citizens are hungry contradicts the Catholic sense of universality. Moreover, competition over the greatest need or the inherent right to help is counterproductive and can leave people powerless. Christians have a duty to young people to introduce them to the needs of all people. God calls young people both to the local soup kitchens and to international missionary work. If they are not introduced to these experiences early in life, they may never consider their options nor hear God's clear invitation.

Young people often come up with unique service ideas as they find their own way to initiate the work that God has inspired within them. I recall a student who arranged to work with UNICEF and became the local contact person for card and gift distribution. She did not envision her work as a mere salesperson; rather, she carried it out with the dignity of saving a life. Having been made aware that the reign of God extends to the entire earth, and that children die of starvation worldwide, she took the situation in hand, contacted UNICEF, and later got to work doing what she could.

Another student from a small, nearby, rural area realized that without a bookmobile of any kind, the elderly and shut-ins of her town had no access to library books. She implemented and managed a mobile library from her car. For a number of hours each week, she selected, delivered, and picked up books for the homebound. After she graduated, the program continued with other volunteers.

Similarly, students living and working with migrant labor families in Florida have always amazed me, as they adapt to living in a culture so different from their own. The students experience the grave prejudice and mistreatment suffered by many of the workers, right here in their own country. Two of these students came back to visit some years later. Recalling their awakening, both reported they had, "never eaten cabbage again without realizing the impact on the poor who provide it for us." When the invitation is extended and the young followers are open, the experience is frequently life-altering.

When The Poor Are Called To Serve

Before enumerating the possibilities for initiating youth into the problems of the world, consider the young person living in some of the previously mentioned situations: the teenage mom, the adolescent in jail as a result of uncontrolled anger, or the troubled student who spends his nights "trespassing" and his days in the classroom. Not only are there students who want to solve the problem, but there are also those who live the problem. The reality that some students live in alcoholic, chaotic homes or even are alcoholics themselves, that some are hungry for food and love, or that some have easy access to gangs and guns and are lonely enough to need them is a stark, but true, reality.

Many educators are unaware of much that happens outside the classroom or religious education program and therefore must accept the challenge to understand more clearly the lives of young people. Imagine a young person eating dinner at a soup kitchen and then going with his or her classmates the next day to serve at the same soup kitchen. More likely, students could have family members or relatives that suffer from domestic violence, alcoholism, or mental illness. Working in a number of settings could raise serious conflict for these students. Keep your antennae for compassion alert and awake at all times in these situations. Compassion demands that educators recognize that not all young people at any given moment are able to meet our demands for service or ministry. Educators must be flexible, loving, and careful not to structure service requirements as a burden or an embarrassment to students.

Service and the Sacraments of Initiation

It is impossible for Christians to read the newspaper, watch television, or listen to anecdotal stories without wondering how the world can survive much longer as it is. Few people have not been touched in some way with the byproducts of violence, disease, poverty, or racism. Helping young people to respond positively to such devastating distress can be overwhelming, even to the seasoned minister. Honoring the graces of the sacraments of initiation, however, is one avenue for those working with high schoolers. The fact that so many parishes require service concurrent with the preparation for the sacrament of Confirmation is not accidental. Sacramental grace is a mighty force for healing the world.

> Sacraments are signs for people to realize, appreciate, and respond to the presence and action of God.

Sacraments are signs for people to realize, appreciate, and respond to the presence and action of God. God does not need sacraments to act, but people need them to fully participate in the action of God. Sacraments of initiation begin something; they bring people to God, familiarizing them with God's presence in the depths of their souls and in the Christian community. Confirmation emphasizes the full presence of the Holy Spirit. It confirms the presence of baptismal gifts, calling all to live a Christian life in a responsible manner. The sacrament of Confirmation also accentuates the unity of the Church in its mission. It is a natural time to help young people develop ministerial roles.

At a time when young people are concerned with finding out who they are, discerning their gifts, and locating their life's direction, the Church offers sacramental signs to reawaken their baptismal identity. Moreover, both the Eucharist and Confirmation grace them for ministry and initiate them into the wider community with its worldwide mission. This is tremendous sustenance in helping young people to embrace their place in the wounded world. Capitalizing on these sacramental connections to fully nourish young people, educators help them advance the Christian mission.

Reflecting on the sacraments of initiation as well as preparing for the sacrament of Confirmation, the young person is helped to make a reverent choice for service that becomes discipleship. Sacramental theology offers a unique distinction between the volunteer and the disciple. Educators have only to offer it and encourage young people in their practice of it; God's grace will take it from there.

Virtues and the Spiritual Development of Youth

Young people also need to be invited to explore virtues as the basis for moral action. Understanding that virtues are practiced habits that demonstrate the inner motivation for good, in union with Christ, will help young people with their natural desire to do good. Young people often wonder what kind of a person they want to be. This is a healthy exploration, and it is fundamental to help young people translate the hope behind this quest.

Young people today admire adults who live their values and principles. Their quest for sincere religion is manifested in their attraction to people who *live* faith, rather than just sitting in church and thinking about it. The teaching of moral goodness through the examples of heroes helps young people practice virtue in their service work.

The societal sins described at the beginning of this chapter would make one think that the virtues of honesty, peace making, respect for creation, and practice of wise judgment are nonexistent. However, these virtues are indeed well and alive in the heroes and heroines of today's youth. Educators need to help the young see and emulate such virtues. Young people are moved when they hear St. Paul's description of unconditional love as patient, kind, and not snobbish. They too aspire to love in this manner.

Young people listen to many songs containing the theme of making the world a better place. Jewel is a singer-songwriter whose songs "Hands" and "Life Uncommon" particularly echo the call to ministry. Adolescents respect her songs because they share honestly about suffering. With a better knowledge of the powerful cultural stories of the young, educators can make effective connections to the Gospel. The universal desire for peace, justice, and harmony is not unique to Christianity. For a recent assignment, several of my students produced music collages to retell the story of Job. I was delighted at the number of A's, as so many students accurately captured Job's faith struggle through current, popular music.

Inviting The Best in our Young People

Young people by nature lead active lives. At a time when their growth is equaled only to that in infancy, is it not alarming that so many of them frequently complain of being bored? Is it not incredible that so many hang out at the mall on weekends with no real purpose? It is revealing that one teenager who recently returned from a missionary trip to Africa with me said, "One of the changes in my life is how uncomfortable I am now at the mall. I just don't see the need for all these things."

Can we not capture a young person's natural tendency towards action? Indeed, it usually does not take much prodding of a young person who by nature loves to be needed. I cannot remember a teenager telling me "no" when I needed help; I can, however, think of many times that I did not think to ask. Jesus extended an invitation to many who seemed unworthy, busy, or otherwise occupied. This should remind everyone that success with the Gospel message is not dependent on age, track record, or skill. The young have to start somewhere and are usually happy to replace Friday night at the mall for an evening at the soup kitchen when offered an enthusiastic invitation.

> Jesus extended an invitation to many who seemed unworthy, busy, or otherwise occupied. This should remind everyone that success with the Gospel message is not dependent on age, track record, or skill.

Young people naturally like having mentors. Feeling needed and special is healthy for adolescents whose lives are complicated by peer pressure. Young people like to have someone new with whom to share activities. The need is great, the fields must be harvested, and the invitation to share experiences with someone who cares is often enough for a young person to commit to a regular service program.

As young people move through high school and on to college, they spend a great deal of time exploring career interests. While I do not advocate service as a way of trying on a career, it is likely that young people will have a tendency to do this. Thus, Catholic education must help them simultaneously consider the Christian call and destiny. While service is not to be used to benefit one's self, there is the likelihood that one will profit from it. The intent and motive, however, will make the difference between discipleship and volunteerism.

Young people must be provided opportunities to consider life choices that involve full-time ministry. I clearly remember a conversation about religious life with students in a classroom setting. "Why," I asked, "do you acknowledge that the mission of the Sisters in this school is wonderful and that they are happy, yet you do not seriously consider religious life yourselves?" One student pointed out, "When we discuss and learn about careers in seminar class, we are not even told about religious life." I submit that the same is true for life ministerial careers such as pastoral ministry. We as a Church are generally failing at introducing life as ministry and mission, somehow expecting that the next generation will already be familiar with it.

The world is broken, and the young have the energy and the desire to *do* good and to *be* good. Educators must put themselves on the line and share ministry with young people. If every person who performs regular service in a parish or school invited a young person to accompany him or her, this would be a strong beginning in initiating the young into discipleship. If every diocesan program or agency mentored one teenager, not only would ministers be formed, but also a knowledge and love of the Church would increase. As the meaning of accompanying young people in ministry and service is explored, consider inviting a young person into your own ministry.

Service as Recompense

Before getting to the intricacies of service programs, one particular item must be noted: Community service as a punishment can be very harmful. When educators intend to teach a lasting lesson, they usually do just that: They create a permanent negative memory. While atonement is an essential aspect of sorrow and forgiveness, and while there may be usefulness in serving those we have hurt, responsibility demands that careful thought precede placing negative, angry people into an already challenging setting.

The ultimate good to be accomplished must be carefully weighed with the obvious limitations. However, this can be done. I stand in awe of one family who worked with an assistant district attorney to get a sentence of "time in a monastery" along with community service, rather than "time in jail" for a young man who took the life of their son. They achieved the goal: reflection and service, not for punishment's sake, but for restoration of the criminal and the community.

In summary, Catholic educators should develop service learning opportunities that join the formative capacities of young people with a strong theological foundation. Such an approach clearly identifies character building efforts from those with added features to deepen spiritual growth.

Chapter 3

Catholic Social Teaching and Service Learning

S   ervice programs rooted in the Church's social teaching fos-
         ter strong discipleship. Christians are intimately bound to
         a God whose care of the poor, concern for human dignity,
         and longing to eliminate injustice are revealed in the life
of Jesus. Catholic-based service learning is predicated on social
justice teaching that is easily accessible.

There is no shortage of ecclesial documents to teach the practice of social justice. Leading the young to service experiences
founded on these documents eliminates social injustice, builds the
Church of the future, and creates a loving kingdom. Initiating
young people into the mystery of God's action is both the primary
purpose and the unique outcome of Catholic service programming.
While young people can accomplish much good with other groups,

it is the Catholic-based service that helps them deepen their relationship with God and continues an ecclesial tradition of prophetic justice.

Foundations of Catholic Service Learning Programs

Catholic social teaching inspires the work of developing disciples. In their June 1998 report, *Sharing Catholic Social Teaching: Challenges and Directions,* the U.S. Catholic Bishops advised Catholic schools, youth ministry programs, and religious education programs to undertake a serious and purposeful effort towards educating the young about Catholic social teaching. The use of the principles of Catholic social teaching in preparation and reflection, coupled with a solid pedagogy, moves ordinary service to a ministerial level.

In their statement, the U.S. Catholic Bishops urged "a renewed commitment to integrate Catholic social teaching into the mainstream of all Catholic educational institutions and programs."[10] Addressing those involved in Catholic education, catechesis, and social ministry, and concluding that there is insufficient knowledge and understanding of social heritage, the bishops advised explicit training in social justice utilizing Church documents. The summary report, written by a task force, concludes:

> After more than two years of assessment and discussion, the task force agreed that although many Catholic educational and catechetical programs excel in communicating Catholic social thought, there are many others that cover the social mission incompletely, indirectly, or not at all. This situation represents a critical problem for the Church's efforts to hand down the faith accurately and in all its dimensions as expressed in the Catechism of the Church. In general, the subgroup determined that there is much interest among Catholic educational, catechetical, and social ministry professionals in incorporating Catholic social teaching into Catholic education programs. However, the extent to which it actually happens is very uneven and is often lacking depth or clarity.[11]

In concluding that social justice activities and service projects do not always include reflection on Catholic social teaching, the task force hit upon the area for which Catholic educators are to be most chastised. The weakness of most service programs is the missed connection between the activity performed and its corresponding Catholic social teaching. Indeed, many young people are pleasantly surprised when the connection is made, as it gives them a newfound pride in their faith. Adequate reflection methods are crucial for a successful understanding.

Essential Elements of Catholic Social Teaching

The Catholic Church has a rich, articulate body of social teaching that is prophetic and instructive. Skillful service programs draw on this rich body, formulating preparatory and reflective strategies to help young people consider their practice in the light of tradition. Virtually every sin and inadequacy a young person observes can be spoken to in Catholic social teaching. The Church's vision is consistent and secure in times of doubt or distress. The Church is unwavering in its promotion of human dignity, just wages and labor practices, reformation of unjust social practices, the duty of nations, recognition of structures that oppress, the distribution of wealth, the relationship of peoples, the root causes of poverty, the life of the marginalized, and the root causes of discrimination. These are just a sampling of the topics in encyclicals and pastoral letters that offer a strong basis for the servanthood to which young people are called.

A summary of essential documents for inclusion in Catholic social teaching with young people is presented here along with extensive excerpts from the World Youth Day messages of Pope John Paul II. Strong in theology, mission, scripture, and ecclesial call, these statements will both encourage educators and communicate church tradition and invitation to the young.

Summary of Relevant Documents

The last one hundred years have produced a rich body of Church documentation useful in curriculum development for service learning. This is an introductory, not exhaustive, list:

Rerum Novarum

Rerum Novarum, "The Condition of Labor," written by Pope Leo XIII in 1891 began a long tradition of papal encyclicals establishing the Church's position in teaching the fundamentals of social justice. At the height of Imperialism, this rudimentary document brought to light the conditions of workers while enumerating their rights. In the midst of pervasive poverty, the Church's stance for the rights of the poor was absolute.

Pope Pius XI in May of 1931 built on *Rerum Novarum* with his encyclical, *Quadragesimo Anno,* "Reconstruction of the Social Order." In responding to the Great Depression, he renewed the message of Leo XIII, tailoring it to the needs of the day. He held that the state is responsible for the social order, noting that capitalism was a precursor to greed. He also focused on the poor, but unlike the previous encyclical, rationalized that systems oppress the poor.

Pope John XXIII

Mater et Magistra, "Christianity and Social Progress," was authored in 1961 by Pope John XXIII. Since tremendous development in the scientific and political worlds had brought dramatic changes, the Pope made clear the growing chasm between the industrialized and non-industrialized nations, making the predicament of the latter evident. He enumerated the disparities and made clear the responsibilities that the wealthier nations had. Two years later, he published *Pacem in Terris,* "Peace on Earth," the first encyclical extended to the non-Catholic world. In a plea for justice, he detailed the social rights and responsibilities that result in lasting peace.

Vatican II documents included *Gaudium et Spes,* "The Church in the Modern World," a call to the "People of God" to transform the world by investigating deeply the changes that both technology and society have had on the growing number of poor. Interestingly, the Pope raised the issue of the loss of traditional values by the younger generation. In fearing that families had become vulnerable to new trends, he called for an increase in the transference of Christian values to the young. Likewise, in light of scientific developments of weaponry, an evaluation of war should be undertaken. This document wrestled with socially relevant concerns as well as with the relationship between church and humanity. It is thus a great resource for service learning curricula.

Pope Paul VI

Pope Paul VI authored *Populorum Progressio,* "The Development of Peoples," in March of 1967. It urged that in response to the teachings of Jesus, people were to nourish and sustain human progress. The Pope characterized progress as necessary to fulfill human potential; our measure is our capacity as God designed us. Like his predecessor, Pope Paul VI believed poverty was the core problem, and he advocated for a world development that would also bring peace. He clarified that violence and revolution were temptations which co-existed with the disparity between the rich and poor. This is notable for young people who seek an understanding of the suffering they might have encountered in such places as Haiti, El Salvador, and other war-torn nations. International development, a subject close to the concerns of today's young people, is also explored in this document.

Four years later with the publication of *Octogesima Adventiens,* "A Call to Action," Pope Paul VI explained the new poor: the elderly, the handicapped, and people made poor as a result of urbanization. Discrimination was a central theme in this document, and a renewed call to political action was brought forth as a way of making necessary systemic changes. The role of the individual Catholic was made clear: All are intended to counter injustice.

On October 26, 1975, Paul VI took up the fundamental aim to make the 20th century Church "ever better fitted for proclaiming the Gospel" in *Evangelii Nuntiandi,* "Evangelization in the Modern World." This was a call to a renewed energy, inherent in people of the Gospel to proclaim liberation from all oppression. In an increasingly de-Christianized environment, we have been challenged to recognize injustice and respond with the liberating good news.

Justice in the World

Another important document for social justice education or service learning background is *Justice in the World.* Published by the United States Synod of Bishops, it focuses on injustices against migrant workers, violations of human rights, torture, and the treatment of political prisoners. In this document, the Church is mandated to be their voice. Liberation continues to be a strong theme, and God is recognized as the true liberator of the oppressed. The phrase "justice is a constitutive dimension of preaching the Gospel" comes from this document.

Pope John Paul II

In 1982, Pope John Paul II focused on "Human Work" in *Laborem Exercens. Rerum Novarum* was now ninety years old, and unemployment had become an increasingly alarming societal problem.

While much of the content was from *Rerum Novarum,* its timeliness was not lost. Criticizing both capitalism and Marxism, the right to own personal property was affirmed, as was the right to common use.

The United States Bishops in *Economic Justice for All* read the signs of the times, challenging the United States economy and its place in international economics. Concerned with Christian values, they elucidated a vision of economic life worthy of Jesus' followers. Notably, this 1986 document called for the Church itself to practice justice in its own undertakings.

Sollicitudo Rei Socialis, "On Social Concern," was written by Pope John Paul II in 1987 to commemorate *Populorum Progressio.* This document declared that the division between east and west continued to be problematic. The global economy at the time reflected the rich as wasting much and the poor as having little. Sinful social structures were identified as a notable cause, and those who perpetuated sinful social structures were reprimanded.

Centesimus Annus, "The Hundred Year," was written to commemorate the hundredth year of *Rerum Novarum.* Written in 1991 by Pope John Paul II, it pointed a finger at atheism as the "fundamental error of socialism." The disregard for humanity and the lack of a transcendent belief about the human were woven into a discussion about communism and capitalism. Although capitalism recognizes the freedom of the human person, its treacheries include a consumeristic society, cheapening the dignity of the person. While it is timely in the context of the Eastern European block, it is timeless in its call to renew and make right our relationship to material possessions.

An important document recommended for thorough study is *The Gospel of Life.* Promulgated by John Paul II in March of 1980, it warns of the pervasive culture of death and encourages a reversal towards a reverence for human life. Young people find this document encouraging and hopeful. Since a strong reverence for the dignity of each person underlies any service on behalf of Christ, the overall tenor and encouragement towards a culture of life is most necessary for today's young people.

Having presented a brief look at the development of the Church's social justice teachings in the last century, a reading of the primary sources is strongly encouraged. Becoming well-versed in the development of the Church's social justice teachings will permit easy referencing and continually inspire both supervisors and service learners to discipleship.

Special Messages for the Youth

Extensive excerpts from the Pope's messages at previous World Youth Days are offered in this next section. Examining the relationship between the Pope and young people is very helpful in establishing service learning that reflects Catholic youth identity. Young people are often unaware of how much the Church cares for them and speaks to them. In his addresses to young people, the Pope comes across as intelligent, loving, and concerned, with a grandfatherly and affectionate tone. Above all, he understands the world much more than young people realize. He is a man who young people can respect; thus, we owe it to them to bring out his words directly.

A slow reading of this section is recommended, perhaps reflecting on only one or two quotes a day over a period of time. This section should be visited again when developing curriculum. Considering these ideas with other staff and faculty, along with young people, increases the ability to distinguish discipleship from mere voluntary service.

In 1985, Pope John Paul II began hosting World Youth Day. In his message for the eighth World Youth Day, he described the purpose of these days as, "providential opportunities to break our journey for a while. They enable young people to examine their deepest aspirations, to heighten their sense of belonging to the Church, and to proclaim their common faith in the crucified and risen Christ with increasing joy and courage. They provide an opportunity for many young people to make bold and enlightened choices which can help steer the further course of history under the powerful but gentle guidance of the Holy Spirit."[12]

Held in various parts of the world, this annual gathering demonstrates the Pope's love for the young people of the Church. The days are thematic and inevitably encourage the young to follow Christ and live lives that are holy in prayer and action. The messages from the past fifteen World Youth Days are readily available through the Vatican Website, http://www.vatican.va. I recommend a full reading of each by educators at every level because they possess ideals deeply rooted in faith, offering the encouragement youth need to follow Christ in formalized religion.

The Theme for the World Youth Day in 1990 was "you have received a spirit of sonship" (Rm. 8:15), and it contains the following powerful statements:

> "You have received a spirit of sonship" (Rm. 8:15). The children of God, that is men and women reborn in Baptism and strengthened in Confirmation, are among the first to be a new civilization, the civilization of truth and love: they are the light of the world and the salt of the earth. (Cf. Mt. 5:13- 16)

> "You have received a spirit of sonship" (Rm. 8:15). How can we fail to be amazed at the heights to which we are called? The human being—a created and limited being, even a sinner—is destined to be a child of God!

> If we call upon God as "Father," we cannot fail to recognize in our neighbor—whoever this may be—a brother or sister who has a right to our love. This is the great commitment for the children of God: working to build a society in which all peoples will live fraternally together. Is not this what the world most needs today? Within nations we can feel the strength of longing for unity that will break down every barrier of indifference and hate. It is especially for you, young people, to take on the great task of building a society where there will be more justice and solidarity.[13]

In 1991, the message of the Pope revolved around the theme "Go into the whole world and proclaim the Gospel" (Mk 16:15). These rich passages help formulate strong Christian service learning programs:

> The Christian vocation is also directed towards the apostolate, towards evangelization, towards mission. All baptized persons are called by Christ to become his apostles in their own personal situations and in the world: "As the father has sent Me, so I send you" (Jn. 20:21).

> Being disciples in Christ is not a private matter. On the contrary, the gift of faith must be shared with others. For this reason Paul writes: "If I preach the Gospel, this is no reason for me to boast, for an obligation has been imposed on me, and woe to me if I do not preach it" (1 Cor 9:16). Moreover, do not forget that faith is strengthened and grows precisely when it is given to others.

The mission lands in which you have been called to work are not necessarily located in distant countries, but can be found throughout the world, even in the everyday situations where you are.

The same world of young people, dear friends, is a mission land for the Church today. Everyone knows the problems which plague the environment in which young people live: the collapse of values, doubt, consumerism, drugs, crime, eroticism, etc. But at the same time every young person has a great thirst for God, even if at times this thirst is hidden behind an attitude of indifference or even hostility.

Proclaiming Christ means above all giving witness to Him with one's life. It is the simplest form of preaching the Gospel and, at the same time, the most effective way available to you. It consists in showing the visible presence of Christ in one's own life by a daily commitment and by making every concrete decision in conformity with the Gospel. Today, the world especially needs believable witnesses. Dear young people, you who love personal authenticity so much and who almost instinctively condemn every type of hypocrisy are able to give a clear and sincere witness to Christ.

Therefore, testify to your faith through your involvement in the world too. A disciple of Christ is never a passive or indifferent observer of what is taking place. On the contrary, he or she feels responsible for transforming social, political, economic, and cultural reality.[14]

At the eighth World Youth Day, the Pope pinpointed clearly the response of the disciple to the hardships they encountered. He adamantly calls young people to life in its fullness in this message:

Our daily experience tells us that life is marked by sin and threatened by death, despite the desire for good which beats in our hearts and the desire for life which courses through our veins. However little heed we pay to ourselves and to the frustrations which life brings us, we discover that everything within us compels us to transcend ourselves, urges us to overcome the temptation of superficiality or despair. It is then that human beings are called to become disciples of that other One who infinitely transcends them, in order to enter at last into true life.[15]

During the ninth and tenth years, the Pope chose John 20:21 for the theme: "As the Father has sent me, so I send you." There are many laudable ideas in this message, including:

The Church entrusts to young people the task of proclaiming to the world the joy which springs from having met Christ. Dear friends, allow yourselves to be drawn to Christ; accept His invitation and follow Him. Go and preach the Good news that redeems (cf. Mt. 28:19); do it with happiness in your hearts and become communicators of hope in a world which is often tempted to despair, communicators of faith in a society which at times seems resigned to disbelief, communicators of love in daily events that are often marked by a mentality of the most unbridled selfishness.

To be able to imitate the disciples, who, overwhelmed by the breath of the Spirit, confidently preached their own faith in the Redeemer who loves everyone and who wants to save everyone, (cf. Acts 2:22-23;32-36) it is necessary to become new people, eradicating the old man within us and allowing ourselves to be totally renewed by the strength of the Lord's Spirit.

His Gospel must become communication and mission. The missionary vocation summons every Christian; it becomes the very essence of every testimony of concrete and living faith. It is a mission which traces its origins from the Father's plan, the plan of love and salvation which is carried out through the power of the Spirit, without which every apostolic initiative is destined to failure.[16]

"Lord to whom shall we go? You have the words of eternal life" is the subject of the eleventh year's message. In this document, the Pope acknowledged the wounds of young people and placed them safely in the arms of a good God who leads them to Himself in others:

> I ask you young people, who naturally and instinctively make your "love of life" the horizon of your dreams and the rainbow of your hopes, to become "prophets of life." Be such by your words and deeds, rebelling against the civilization of selfishness that often considers the human person a means rather than an end, sacrificing its dignity and feelings in the name of mere profit. Do so by concretely helping those who need you and who perhaps, without your help, would be tempted to resign themselves in despair.
>
> By conforming your daily life to the Gospel of the one Teacher who has "the words of eternal life," you will be able to become genuine workers for justice, following the commandment which makes life the new "frontier" of Christian witness. This is the law for transforming the world (cf. Gaudium et spes, n. 38).

The way Jesus shows you is not easy. Rather, it is like a path winding up a mountain. Do not lose heart! The steeper the road, the faster it rises towards ever wider horizons.

Remember the master's warning: "I was hungry and you gave me food, I was thirsty and you gave me drink, I was a stranger and you welcomed me, I was naked and you clothed me, I was sick and you visited me, I was in prison and you came to me" (Mt. 25:25-36). We must put the "new commandment" into practice (Jn 13:34).

Thus we will oppose what today seems to be the "disintegration of civilization," in order vigorously to reaffirm the "civilization of love" which alone can open to the men of our time horizons of true peace and lasting justice in lawfulness and solidarity.[17]

On the occasion of the twelfth World Youth Day, Pope John Paul II focused on John's words: "Teacher, where are you staying? Come and see." This message should be read and studied in its entirety for its value in helping the young maintain the identity of disciple while performing service:

Dear young people, like the first disciples, follow Jesus! Do not be afraid to draw near to Him, to cross the threshold of His dwelling, to speak with Him, face to face, as you talk with a friend (cf. Ex. 33:11). Do not be afraid of the new life He is offering. He himself makes it possible for you to receive that life and practice it, with the help of His grace and the gift of His Spirit.

It is true: Jesus is a demanding friend. He points to lofty goals; He asks us to go out of ourselves in order to meet Him, entrusting to Him our whole life, "Whoever loses his life for My sake and that of the Gospel will save it" (Mk. 8:35). The proposal may seem difficult, and in some cases, frightening. But—I ask you—is it better to be resigned to a life without ideals, to a world made in our image and likeness, or rather, generously seek truth, goodness, justice, working for a world that reflects the beauty of God, even at the cost of facing the trials it may involve?

Come and see. You will meet Jesus where men and women are suffering and hoping: in the little villages, scattered across the continents, and seemingly on the fringe of history, as Nazareth was when God sent His Angel to Mary; in the huge metropolises, where millions of human beings live often as strangers. In reality, every human being is a "fellow citizen of Christ."

Jesus is living next to you, in the brothers and sisters with whom you share your daily existence. His visage is that of the poorest, of the marginalized who, not infrequently, are victims of an unjust model of development, in which profit is given first place and the human being is made a means rather than an end. Jesus' dwelling is wherever a person is suffering because rights are denied, hopes betrayed, anxieties ignored. There in the midst of humankind, is the dwelling of Christ, who asks you to dry every tear in his name, and to remind whoever feels lonely that no one whose hope is placed in Him is ever alone. (Cf. Mt. 25:31-6)

But how are you to be recognized as true Disciples of Christ? By the fact that you have "love for one another" (Jn 13:35) after the example of His love; a love that is freely given, infinitely patient and denied to no one (cf. 1 Cor. 13:4-7). Fidelity to the new commandment will be the guarantee that you are consistent with respect to what you are proclaiming. This is the great "novelty" which can amaze a world that, unfortunately, is still torn and divided by violent conflicts that at times are clearly evident, at times subtle and hidden. In this world, you are called to live fraternally, not as a utopia but as a real possibility; in this society, you are called, as true missionaries of Christ, to build the civilization of love.[18]

At the Youth Jubilee in August of 2000, the Pope continued his message with the theme: "The Word became flesh and dwelt among us" (Jn. 1:14):

Young people of every continent, do not be afraid to be the saints of the new millennium! Be contemplative, love prayer, be coherent with your faith and generous in the service of your brothers and sisters, be active members of the Church and builders of peace. To succeed in this demanding project of life, continue to listen to His Word, draw strength from the sacraments, especially the Eucharist and Penance. The Lord wants you to be intrepid apostles of His Gospel and builders of a new humanity.[19]

During his homily at the closing liturgy, the Pope reaffirmed the connection between sacramental grace and the call to service:

To celebrate the Eucharist, "to eat His flesh and drink His blood," means to accept the wisdom of the Cross and the path of service. It means that we signal our willingness to sacrifice ourselves for others, as Christ has done. Our society desperately needs this sign, and young people need it even more so, tempted as they often are by the illusion of an easy and comfortable life, by drugs and pleasure-seeking, only to find themselves in a spiral of despair, meaninglessness, and violence. It is urgent to change direction and to turn to Christ. This is the way of justice, solidarity, and commitment to building a society and a future worthy of the human person.

Live the Eucharist by testifying to God's love for every person.[20]

During a vigil prayer the evening before, the Pope challenged youth to respond to the age-old question: "But who do you say that I am?" (Mt. 16:15). In probing the significance of the exchange between the disciples and Jesus, the Pope asked the young people: "What is the meaning of this dialogue? Why does Jesus want to know what people think about Him? Why does He want to know what His disciples think of Him?"

> "It is Jesus who stirs in you the desire to do something great with your lives, the will to follow an ideal, the refusal to allow yourselves to be grounded down by mediocrity, the courage to commit yourselves humbly and patiently to improving yourselves and your society, making the world more human and more fraternal."

Jesus wants his disciples to become aware of what is hidden in their own minds and hearts and to give voice to their conviction. At the same time, however, He knows that the judgment they will express will not be theirs alone, because it will reveal what God has poured into their heart by the grace of faith.[21]

The Pope further strengthened the young with these beautiful words:

It is Jesus in fact that you seek when you dream of happiness; He is waiting for you when nothing else you find satisfies you; He is the beauty to which you are so attracted; it is He who provokes you with that thirst for fullness that will not let you settle for compromise; it is He who urges you to shed the masks of a false life; it is He who reads in your hearts your most genuine choices;

the choices that others try to stifle. It is Jesus who stirs in you the desire to do something great with your lives, the will to follow an ideal, the refusal to allow yourselves to be grounded down by mediocrity, the courage to commit yourselves humbly and patiently to improving yourselves and your society, making the world more human and more fraternal.

Dear young people, in these noble undertakings you are not alone. With you there are families, communities, there are your priests and teachers, there are so many of you who in the depths of your hearts never weary of loving Christ and believing in Him. In the struggle against sin, you are not alone; so many like you are struggling and through the Lord's grace are winning

Dear friends, at the dawn of the millennium, I see in you the "morning watchmen" (cf. Is 21:11-12).

Dear young people of the century now beginning, in saying "yes"to Christ, you say "yes" to all your noblest ideals. I pray that He will reign in your hearts and in all of humanity in the new century and the new millennium. Have no fear of entrusting yourselves to Him! He will guide you, He will grant you the strength to follow Him every day and in every situation.[22]

Lest there is any doubt remaining regarding the Pope's deep affection and concern for the young of the Church, reflect on his closing words at the World Youth Day for the Jubilee: "At the end of this World Youth Day, as I look at you now, at your young faces, at your genuine enthusiasm, from the depths of my heart I want to give thanks to God for the gift of youth, which continues to be present in the Church and in the world because of you."[23]

Developing Gospel Servants: Preparation

The indispensable relationship between service activity and Christian discipleship has been clearly established. Service programs of all varieties struggle to provide strong preparation and meaningful reflection. Whatever the pedagogical motive or expressed intended outcomes, these two components determine success, failure, or mediocrity in service programming.

What specific elements create disciples? In addition to guidance concerning skills and specific tasks to be performed, Gospel-based service learning includes:

- understanding the call to love as Jesus loved.
- an appreciation of the population being served as God's beloved.
- rootedness in the philosophy and goals of Catholic social teaching.
- an appreciation of the purpose of the work and the dignity of one's contribution.
- understanding the systematic and root causes of the problems being addressed.
- applying appropriate social justice documents of the Church.
- living the call from Pope John Paul II to the young to live as Christ's disciples.

The importance of utilizing Church documents as a resource for interpreting these elements cannot be overemphasized. The social justice documents are the explicit curriculum for a solid comprehension of the Gospel call. Moreover, Catholic social teaching informs the disciple about the population served with suitable philosophies and goals. Being well acquainted with Catholic social teaching documents helps students realize the purpose and dignity of their work, as well as the root causes of social problems. The youth should be encouraged to search the primary sources themselves. This is important in molding Catholics that assume ongoing responsibility for knowing what the Church is really saying, not what the secular media reports.

A solid preparation creates willing, able, and confident participants. Volunteers of any age have anxiety about new situations and oftentimes lack the confidence to "pitch right in" for fear of doing something wrong. Young people are best prepared to serve as Jesus did when solid comprehension supports personal confidence. For a more extensive look at justice education, one should read Thomas Groome's chapter, "A Faith that Does Justice: Beyond the Scales," found in his encyclopedic treatment of Christian service, *Educating for Life*. This chapter is a must read for administrators, educators, and parents who wish to help young people develop in the area of justice.

Developing Servants of the Gospel: Reflection

Reflecting on one's experience can take many forms, but expected outcomes include:

- an appreciation for the sacredness of belonging to the family of God.
- rejoicing in the dignity of each human as God's image (including one's self).
- an appreciation for God's grace acting in one's life.
- grasping the Church's call to social justice and the service site's response.
- articulating the experience as a Gospel event.

The most common format for reflecting on service experiences is the journal. It can be an even more effective method when sentence starters are given. Sentence starters should be designed towards the intended outcome. Some openers that my students have used effectively in the past include: "I met Christ today when..." "I recognized the Church's understanding of Love (Justice, Peace, Solidarity, Dignity, etc.) enacted when...." "If I could speak about my service experience at a Church homily, I would tell others that...." "Being a part of the people of God was clear to me when..." Another approach might include writing reflection papers on some of the Pope's statements presented earlier in this chapter or using these statements to caption a photo journal of the service experience.

Students reflect well with photo journals, song collages, short skits, and other creative methods. It is very important that young people tell others what the experience has meant to them. It is sharing their own adventure with the "Good News"; it is Jesus alive and living the Word in them. Sharing the "Good News" gives them dignity in the family of God.

Mandatory Service, An Oxymoron?

Many schools and parishes have struggled with the concept of mandatory service. Can service or volunteering be made mandatory and still maintain the integrity of its charitable nature? Is it Gospel driven if it is not a choice? These are really not questions for a program that is Christian in nature. For to be Christian is to serve. Baptism mandates service in our everyday living. Jesus modeled a life of serving others and commands us to follow His example. Christian formation is the aim of Catholic education whether in schools, parishes, or youth ministry programs. One could never think of forming a Christian without saturating them with the tradition and practice of social justice. It would not only weaken the Christian tradition, it would eliminate its substance.

Indeed, mandatory service should be an aspect of all Christian initiation and formation. Programs such as the Rite of Christian Initiation of Adults (RCIA) should include an experience of service to make clear to the initiate that an option for the poor and a daily living of Catholic social teaching is obligatory. It has been the experience of many youth educators that students, while they were not happy about being told they must do service, were in the end grateful for the experience.

It is clearly revealed in Jesus' life and ministry, in the Gospels, and in Catholic tradition that service is not an added extra; rather, it is primary. In an age when it seems that civic responsibility has weakened, moral norms have been abandoned, and so many are hungry for human contact, service learning is actually an easy sell. However, without a strong foundation in Catholic social teaching, young people simply experience feeling good for doing good. Service learning is key to forming mature and knowledgeable Catholics who appreciate their social justice heritage and respond actively to the call "to build a civilization of love."

Chapter 4

Balancing Pedagogy and Ministry

Service-Learning History

An experiential, service-oriented curriculum is not a new concept. The current practice of service learning has its foundation in the last century in a variety of pedagogical practices. The task of the Catholic educator in service education is to balance good pedagogical process and Gospel directives. This chapter explores service learning ideas in current educational practice and suggests ways to use this theory effectively without betraying the fundamental role of developing disciples.

Educational theory has long grasped that learning is enhanced by experience and that information is magnified when put to immediate and practical use. Aristotle's *Public Education* first introduced the theory of character education. "Progressive education" for the purpose of "building a new social order" was a phrase used in 1932 by Columbia professor George S. Counts. Programs such as the Civilian Conservation Camp in the 1930's, VISTA, the Peace Corps, and the current, widespread Americorps programs have likewise made an impact on the development of service programs in secondary schools. These programs succeed at providing the "hands-on" experiences that form good citizens, while the needs in such areas as racism, poverty, abuse, and literacy are met. The realization that these programs provide a good instructive model has led, in part, to the adaptation of this methodology at the primary and secondary school levels. The position that it is the school's role to teach character education and to produce good citizens has contributed to a proliferation of community service learning materials.

In more recent years, the Community Service Act has influenced service learning. In 1990, The Federal National and Community Service Act created a commission to "explore and test innovative ways to renew the ethic of civic responsibility;" subsequently, in 1993, the Act created a Corporation for National and Community Service bringing several service groups together. The National Service-Learning Clearinghouse was formed to establish an outlet for students K-12 to obtain assistance in developing service materials and programs. By 1994, more than $30 million government dollars had been appropriated to service learning. This funding continues through programs like Literacy America and Americorps as well as programs at the primary and secondary levels. Coordinators for the various regions of the country oversee this funding which is available to all levels of education. The National Corporation maintains a website called Learn and Serve (www.cns. gov/learn/about/service_learning.html), which has standards, definitions, related websites, and a clearinghouse for local and national information. The best way to employ these resources is to contact the state Department of Education and determine who is responsible locally for allocating the resources. Many states offer excellent training programs in service learning using these national dollars.

Project, Programs, and Variety in Service Learning

Known as "character education," "community service," "service learning," "volunteer work," or "experiential learning," the terminology surrounding this explosion has created as much confusion as good will. "Service learning" typically refers to programs that combine community need with the school's already established curriculum. As such, the intended outcome is related to curriculum objectives; it is designed and mandated through the educational system.

"Community service" is not always linked to educational objectives. Although community service should always enhance a person's growth, it is not always the intended purpose. It can simply meet a community need. Thus, community service can differ from service learning both in design and intent. Community service programs are typically associated with courts, welfare systems, and groups such as the Girls and Boys Clubs of America. They aim to build character or help people find their usefulness in society. "Service learning," however, is typically linked to schools or other formal educational endeavors and is related to specific curriculum guidelines. As such, it is constructed with both implicit and explicit educational objectives.

An important difference in service learning is found in projects versus programs. The intent and design of a project usually differs from a program. Projects and programs have substantial differences in goals, training, time commitment, and reflection. Service programs typically involve ongoing experiences that contain recurring elements of investigation, analysis, action, and reflection. These differ from the occasional project, integral to the curriculum but intended to be of short duration with a single, specific purpose. Also, designed to analyze, act, and reflect, the scope of singular activities is limited, more typically involving direct service without aims towards systemic change.

A "program" might involve a student visiting the same site for a two-year period, but a "project" with the science class more likely involves a cleanup day while studying the environment. One might introduce students to service with a shared project and then progress to a longer commitment that provides regular contact over a long period of time. An ongoing relationship with a single site lends itself to objectives that need a longer duration such as analyzing the plight of the poor and taking action for systemic change. The intended outcome differs vastly from the single project of visiting a nursing home at the holidays. Both must be tied appropriately to the mission and objectives at hand. Community service and service learning are equally useful experiences for developing the young person. Any type of service experience enhances expertly executed Catholic education.

The nature of many Catholic school mission statements, along with the shared goal to develop disciples, lend the Catholic educational system to service programs, i.e., ongoing planned activities tied to curriculum and mission. Consequently, Catholic education is compelled to include intentionally designed, curriculum-driven, service learning programs and projects to meet immediate needs in the community. For example, during the Kosovo crisis, one of my students suggested a clothing drive for refugees. This led to a religion class of making cloth diapers for the many infants whose families were homeless and in refugee camps. This singular activity met an important need and was well within the mission of the school to prepare students for their role as Christians. The global nature of this project, the ability to learn about a cultural heritage, and the need met for families in the camps were all important factors considered in supporting this student's suggestion.

Public schools, clubs, and court mandated programs suffice on service focused on good citizenship. Catholic education mandates service learning with clear Gospel directives. Catholic educators are obliged to keep their work steeped in social justice. This simplifies the task for the framework and is readily accessible in Church documents on social teaching and in the Gospel tradition.

CRITICAL ELEMENTS FOR CATHOLIC CURRICULUM DEVELOPMENT

There are many resources available for educators, and while it is not this book's intent to re-teach either the elements of curriculum development or Catholic social teaching, it is to be emphasized that these remain the basis for effective service learning experiences. Curricula without a primary social justice component, no matter how intricate or well developed, are not a good choice for the Catholic educator. Unfortunately, some Catholic educators have resorted to using materials that, although solid for public education, lack the very components that build discipleship. These programs lack the social justice teaching of the Church and keep spirituality out of the reflection components. Curricula need to have these key components.

Whatever the duration or type of service, good pedagogical process demands solid preparation and sufficient reflection. Preparing the young person to participate in any learning experience requires clearly articulated objectives, a good introduction to the anticipated situation, an awareness of the circumstance in the larger context, an examination of existing possibilities and potential, and a review of procedures and policies that could affect participation and outcome. Lack of preparation is the fundamental reason many lesson plans fail, both in and out of the classroom. There is a more pressing need in community service learning to anticipate the possibilities and outcomes. Preparation can help eliminate problems associated with taking the classroom into the community. There are many new things for each party to consider, not the least being the role of a supervisor whose expectations are then joined to the teacher's. A good preparation begins with a clearly articulated set of objectives that the student, supervisor, and teacher understand and focus on throughout the service learning process.

> *Essential to the successful pedagogical process is a reflection method that helps the participant explore the significance and meaning of the experience.*

Essential to the successful pedagogical process is a reflection method that helps the participant explore the significance and meaning of the experience. Reflection is also useful to determine if the stated objectives and outcomes have been realized. Christians have a unique definition of success, and therefore it is very important to be explicit in helping young people reflect with this in mind. "God's ways are not our ways," and while the Cross seemed in the eyes of many to be foolish, it is for Christians the very core of their belief and practice. The nature of salvific action is one to consider with young people as they encounter the pain of the world. Herein, there is a real challenge to harmonize pedagogical and Gospel success. Jesus' mandates are in conflict with the world's idea of success. Followers of Christ must not compromise with an evaluative process outside the Gospel tradition.

It cannot be expected that everything will work to perfection, nor should success be measured by feeling good. People are more experienced at measuring the pedagogical process. In the area of evaluating discipleship, a new standard must be used. This is an area in which Catholic educators are far less prepared. Nevertheless, Catholic educators should hold themselves to quality standards objectively assessed in both educational pedagogy and Gospel mandate.

Since most Catholic schools have a mission statement frequently related to a congregational mission, an important element in the design and evaluation of service learning begins with analyzing service in light of the school's mission statement. While it indicates most clearly the school's intended focus, it is often not consulted. The mission statement is the school's framework for ministerial outreach. Service programs should reflect its philosophy and its goals.

Measuring Curriculum Effectiveness

In March of 1995, The Alliance for Service Learning in Education Reform articulated clear ideals for service learning. These can be adapted to fit an individual institution in measuring the effectiveness of service learning:

- Effective service learning efforts strengthen service and academic learning.
- Model service learning provides concrete opportunities for youth to learn new skills, to think critically, and to test new roles in an environment that encourages risk-taking and rewards competence.
- Preparation and reflection are essential elements in service learning.
- Youths' efforts are recognized by those served, including their peers, the school, and the community.
- Youth are involved in the planning.
- The service students perform makes a meaningful contribution to the community.
- Effective service learning integrates systematic formative and summative evaluation.
- Service learning connects the school or sponsoring organizations and the community in new and positive ways.
- Service learning is understood and supported as an integral element in the life of a school or sponsoring organization and the community.

- Skilled adult guidance and supervision are essential to the success of service learning.
- Pre-service training, orientation, and staff development that include the philosophy and methodology of service learning best ensure that program quality and continuity are maintained. [24]

Creating the "Ah Ha" Moment

Educators are always delighted by the "Ah Ha" moments. These grace-filled moments when the learner makes a discriminating connection to the material are common to service learning. Educators can help create these moments with solid preparation. The "Ah Ha" experience is comparable to the religious experience. It is characterized by awareness which goes beyond the intellectual truth. The connection of a number of ideas, a reasoned understanding, a glimpse of a new possibility, the excitement of evidence confirming the hunch that was in the back of one's mind—these are all experiences of the "Ah Ha" moment. Jesus was a master at producing "Ah Ha" moments. When Nicodemus finally understood light and dark as being analogous to himself and when the Samaritan women understood not only the nature of a falsehood but also the reality of truth, triumphant "Ah Ha" moments were fostered by Jesus, the teacher.

Service learning provides a fitting environment for "Ah Ha" moments. The practicality, spontaneity, and freedom found in service invite young people to see with new eyes. A different environment allows them to leave schoolwork behind. Without the burden of passing or failing, those who struggle academically can perceive new strengths in themselves and develop a more positive self-esteem. Often, when a student experiences these moments, teachers are not present to observe them. Teachers might read about them in a journal or hear about them when a student rushes in before school to tell an exciting story. The religious experience is much the same. Each person is given daily grace to accept the invitation of a God who loves all people unconditionally and constantly calls everyone deeper into that love. All have received insights about God that were so simple that they wondered why they did not realize these before. This kind of recognition offers more than cognitive understanding; it begins to entertain a deeper relationship with the mystery of God.

The religious experience, God's call to love in action, is innate in each person, especially students. It is ready to be cultivated in service learning. The new understanding of the world that awaits them, cultivated as they serve, is an entry to the natural search for God. Educators are charged with helping them to grasp this great mystery.

While working with the young in poor countries, I delight at their openness to doing things in a different way. For example, students who work in Haiti inevitably see a connection between the water wasted on a 20-minute shower at home and the lack of this basic resource in a place like Haiti. Their steadfast will in making change when they returned home confirms that the "Ah Ha" moment had been experienced. These are religious in nature as young people resolve to live the Gospel mandate to share the earth's resources more equitably. Herein, the pedagogical process of the "Ah Ha" moment supports and enlivens personal growth that reflects the social teaching of the Church.

Formative Elements in Curriculum Design, Intended to Foster Disciples

Catholic education has long been known for strong pedagogy and successful teaching/learning methods. As educators develop service learning programs to enhance Catholic school curricula, they need to think about considerations not found in the current literature on service learning. The goal to form disciples requires special elements that help young people achieve ministerial growth. Curriculum design should insure that:

- the learner understands and appreciates the action of God in the service learning experience.
- the learner is aware of the skills, talents, and gifts needed to perform Christian service, including sacramental graces and nourishment.
- the learner is aware of the greater context of the situation, both from a worldly and religious perspective.
- the objectives for the service experience are clear, can be measured by the learner and supervisor, and are rooted in Catholic social teaching.
- the reflection process leads to celebration and prayer.

- the recipients are the poor, the outcast, and the marginalized.

Educators will do well to keep a balance between a vision of faith and a competent educational methodology. Before turning to the practical daily concerns of service learning, keep in mind that this endeavor is first and foremost God's work.

> If the Lord does not build the house, the builders work in vain.
> If the Lord does not watch over the city, the guards watch in vain.
> How foolish to rise early and slave until night for bread.
> Those who please God receive as much even while they sleep
> (Psalm 127:1-2).

John Dewey once remarked, "Perhaps the greatest of all pedagogical fallacies is that people learn the thing they are studying at the time they are studying it." This is a humbling reminder that the most eloquent lesson plan will be ineffective until such time as the learner is ready and able to understand. Even with the Lord building the house, people are limited in their capacity to affect immediate change or understanding. With this humility, one should always consider the necessary pedagogical elements for service learning.

If the Lord does not build the house, the builders work in vain. If the Lord does not watch over the city, the guards watch in vain.

How foolish to rise early and slave until night for bread. Those who please God receive as much even while they sleep (Psalm 127:1-2).

Shared Praxis: A Curriculum Model for Service Learning

A shared praxis methodology reflects pedagogical movement from awakening to experiencing, from reflection to discovering a faith story, from discovery to owning the faith and responding in faith. These movements are done in a dance rather than a march. The steps are not always experienced sequentially. Curricula can be formulated with the steps in sequence, but God and the learner sometimes have other plans. Some of the best learning situations have been wrought from responding in faith and then looking back. As such, service learning experiences can either confirm faith or awaken it; it can be the focusing activity or the evaluative portion of learning.

In the early 1990's, while teaching a course to seniors in high school, I utilized shared praxis. During the last two months of my students' junior year, I worked with them in choosing an activity which would serve as the educational focus for *Peace through Justice*. During the summer, a committee wrote up the project, applied for funding to support it, and prepared a full introduction for the rest of the class. When the course began in the fall of their senior year, 61 young women went full force into the praxis method or what I then called "service learning." Calling their project ASAP (A School Age Program About Substance Abuse Problems Alerting Students About Prevention), these seniors embarked wholeheartedly on providing a performing and visual arts program in one of the poorest schools in the city. I offer their reflections later to demonstrate the usefulness of a shared praxis model in constructing a curriculum for service learning.

Primarily, the young women involved in this project were privileged and had little previous contact with the poor. Ninety-two percent of the families we worked with fell below the government's definition of poverty. While doing a project was not a choice for the students, they determined the site and subject of their work. Since funding had cut the visual and performing arts programming from the public schools that year, the students' decision was to supply some type of arts experience. Coming to know and understand the population they served helped these students to select the drug abuse prevention content.

The shared praxis method that was used contained the following movements:

- Focusing activity
- Experiencing life
- Reflecting together
- Discovering the faith story
- Owning the faith
- Responding in faith

The *focusing activity* is that moment that attracts the individual's attention to the justice issue and builds personal involvement. Some students describe this moment as a time earlier in their lives when they saw a drug addicted person on the street, or when they were living with their own alcoholic parent. Many students had not yet realized the connection between economics and drug or alcohol addiction. For at least three students, writing the project grant was the focusing activity. For others, it was choosing the committee on which they would serve, and for still others, it was the films, speakers, and personal stories of classmates. One girl's awareness came with her direct involvement with the children. The personal impact was obvious; she was building the personal involvement required by the focusing activity:

> *Our first day was a bit of a shock. It seemed that the children had more experience with drugs and alcohol than we had. It was very depressing to see this. I also experienced that many of the children did not seem to have the proper education at this point in their lives. A girl just yesterday asked me how to spell "drugs."*

In *experiencing life*, the next movement, students explored personal and local community occurrences of injustice. They explored what they knew, what they felt, and what their actions meant. A sampling of this experience is found in the words of one student who speaks about what it was like to attend an Alcoholics Anonymous meeting, and of another who reflects on her first day of teaching fourth graders:

> *There were all kinds of people at this large meeting. To me, they looked like anyone else. I now have a strong admiration for recovering addicts. I had never thought before about how difficult it must be to stop drinking. However, when I listened to the speakers, I learned that recovery is an ongoing struggle. I do not feel that these people are any different from anyone else except for the fact that they are trying hard to overcome a disease.*

> *The experience that touched me the most was on the first day we went to teach. Kathleen and I started to ask the children true and false questions about drugs and alcohol. The children did pretty well in answering the questions, but they had many of their own comments to share with us. One boy told us how his uncle was an alcoholic and had just passed away. Another boy explained that he sees a drunken man walk through his neighborhood often. A girl told us that there are needles all over her neighborhood. Many other children told us stories of that nature also. This was very devastating to listen to. It shocked me because I began to realize that these children had more experience with drugs and alcohol than I did. With all of their comments, it showed me that they have a lot of knowledge about the subject, but they still do not*

understand what is going on in their society. It made me extremely sad to see that these children had to go through this at such a young age and not realize what was going on.

Reflecting together, the next movement, includes expanding understanding and broadening one's perspectives in light of the experience of the wider community. The words of two student leaders of the project show the fruit of shared reflection and the value of stepping back to see the wider picture:

Through this experience, I have learned many things I consider valuable as a senior heading out into the "real world." The first thing I have learned is that sometimes you have to look beyond the things you don't really like to do, to discover the good that has really been done. Once I get beyond complaining and really think about what I am doing, I realize what I am learning, how I am serving, and how I am helping the second graders.

When Mrs. Wilson took control of my lesson, I automatically disliked her because she did not let me do what I wanted. I should have approached her about it; I should have talked with her about the situation. The major point is that I have to be more open to constructive criticism. I have learned to speak up for myself, not to judge others, and to look beyond dislikes to see the joy we bring to other people that are touched in our lives.

By sharing stories in class, I learned that the horror stories that we are told in school are happening right down the street from me. I guess I knew that before, but this project really brought the fact home to me.

In the process of *discovering the faith story*, the individual and the group listen to the faith story and to the faith community. The clearest example of this is found in a class reflection on the parable of the vineyard. The class' struggle involved the age-old problem of equality and fairness. It eventually surfaced that some students were working harder than others, and since they were grading themselves, it greatly disturbed some that those who "did very little" could give themselves "an A." Some discovered authentic justice in the faith story, others remained adamant and angry. Here is a sampling of their insights:

Jesus preached about God's Kingdom to the already pious and to sinners. If both accepted his preaching, both would be granted an equal share in God's Kingdom regardless of their prior past. With Project ASAP, fairness is not based on equality. Fairness is situational. I believe that those who commit themselves partially or entirely to works of peace and justice have received a special calling.

I guess what I am trying to say is that Jesus would tell me that the same people are always doing everything in the work of peace and justice, because they have discovered that they benefit as much from their work as the object of their work.

It is difficult for us to accept the idea that everyone deserves equal reward for work accomplished—however great or small. I think society contradicts the parable of the vineyard by dictating that a larger output merits a larger reward. It is frustrating that the generous and understanding view of the parable cannot satisfy society's thirst for growth and advancement.

One insight the parable gives me about ASAP is that not everyone understands generosity.

When thinking about what Jesus would say about some people doing more work than others, I cannot help but think of the story of Jesus' visit to Martha and Mary. One of the sisters prepared dinner and cleaned the house because they were having a guest, Jesus. While the other, although she appeared lazy, was actually listening to everything Jesus had to say. When the hard-working sister complained, Jesus told her that the other was accomplishing more by listening and she should do the same. This story makes me feel as though Jesus would respond by saying that we should not be concerned with what others are doing, but know that what you are doing is a good thing even if it is different from someone else.

Notice the assortment of discoveries, each a valuable and worthy lesson in itself. In sharing the faith story, like any other Gospel-sharing group, students glean varying but important messages.

In coming to *own their faith*, students are challenged to consider the implications of the faith story for their lives and for the community. This movement also involves exploring possible *faith responses,* which is the final movement. Sophia was involved in teaching a kindergarten class. In this class, a little girl disclosed to the teacher (unbeknownst to Sophia) that her mother was shooting up heroin in front of her. As a result of this disclosure, an investigation ensued and the child was removed from her home. Sophia was teaching the class when this took place, but appeared unfazed at the time of the incident. Sophia was a religious education teacher in her parish and possessed a great deal of "faith knowledge," but did not regularly openly share her faith. Evaluating her experience, however, Sophia came to a new understanding about the work of justice and peace in her faith:

> As I said before, when I first started teaching, I had neutral feelings about the whole thing. As you recall, there was an incident in the kindergarten where a girl was taken from her home and placed in a foster home because of a substance abuse problem. At first I had no reaction. It happened. There was no dwelling on it. After a while, though, I really started to think about it and kept replaying it in my mind. What did that little girl feel like? This was the biggest turning point for me. I actually started looking at the whole incident from different perspectives, not just my own. Even now when I think about it, I can't believe how serious it all was and how I just shrugged it off, as if it never happened. The whole experience touched me. My eyes are being opened to the whole meaning of what is going on and how I am doing the work of peace and justice.

Another student used the pastoral circle, a reflection-action model, to describe her growth:

> After much thought, I have decided that I began my revolution around the pastoral circle in the traditional starting place—involvement. I consider my first meeting at the school my initiation into the project. Walking through the hallways, listening to the principal talk about the poverty and abuse among his students and witnessing firsthand the numerous and desperate needs of the school itself, I became involved. I started to see distant issues from a different point of view and could no longer say or think about the words "substance abuse" without thinking of the children and families at the school.
>
> If possible, my movement in the pastoral circle led me into action and exploration at the same time. While we were writing the grant, I learned not only about the rate of substance abuse in our community, but also about the disrespect with which young people are constantly treated. I became more aware of the many justice issues that face us and of the difficulty of coming together to change what is so obviously wrong. I definitely believe that I experienced

both action and exploration simultaneously without breaking the pastoral circle. As we discussed in class, it is possible to connect any of the four steps by simply drawing a line through the center of the circle. This possibility reinforces the idea that all aspects of peace and justice are interconnected and that one can move freely about the pastoral circle.

For me, reflection happened at several points along the journey. In a very subtle way, every time someone asked me about our efforts with the project, I would inevitably think about what we were doing in relation to what I have been taught in my life. People's comments and opinions gave me more to ponder. Their praises affirmed my belief in a universal desire for justice; their skepticism made me wonder what I could do to make ASAP better or more effective. Just as questions provoked reflection, self-evaluations in class forced me to look at my participation in the project. Never once did my reflection lead me to believe that ASAP was doing the wrong thing. It seems that we found ASAP to be not only an excellent way to study peace and justice, but we saw where ASAP was in unison with our values and principles and where it was not.

The students who completed this project were one of many groups to pass through my *Peace through Justice* class using this model. Their reflections demonstrate a praxis model. This is only one way to formulate a service curriculum. It is uniquely ministerial in its outreach to the poor and in its praxis model. The more closely ministry and learning outcomes are held together, the more successful educators are at forming disciples and practicing good pedagogical process.

Chapter 5

Challenges to Off-Site Learning Programs

Service Learning Challenges

Service learning is not without struggles and obstacles. It is a lot of work! Expanding the curriculum beyond the classroom poses unique challenges. This chapter explores some of the common difficulties experienced in selecting, building, and maintaining ongoing programs that take place outside of the school or parish. Securing quality sites takes a bit of recruiting and some extra time; however, it also provides lively and solid experiences.

Luke's Gospel tells us that Jesus sent his disciples out two by two with specific instructions and careful direction. The Gospel does not clarify how much training they had or how confident they felt about meeting the myriad of needs they would encounter. While not anticipating every need for them, Jesus did set some structure as they approached their work. Service program coordinators must anticipate probable issues and uncertainties and give adequate direction, while leaving room for the work of the Holy Spirit and the growth of the young people.

Service Sites

Keeping in mind the innumerable needs of service sites, the busy environment of many social service agencies, and the spontaneous lifestyle of young people, educators should anticipate and structure service requirements accordingly. Helping to eliminate some of the foreseeable schedule and planning problems is one way to support service sites. This might sound a bit simplistic. However, many students fail to call to report that they are not coming to their service assignment, even when they have been scheduled far in advance. In their growing understanding of responsibility, the young volunteer must come to realize the impact they have on others when they do not show up. When students are trained that open, honest, and timely communication is a part of loving service, the significance of the agency's need is conveyed, the school's good name is protected, and the young person learns the importance of a commitment.

Good preparation for a disciple includes both practical training and spiritual enrichment. The best case scenario for a student site selection process might look like this: Having a cogent understanding of the Church, the school, or parish mission to the poor and having prayed and discerned about where they might best serve the needs of the community, the volunteer visits several sites. An evaluation sheet assessing practical and spiritual considerations with clearly stated pedagogical objectives guides them as they look at a potential placement. Prayer and reflection—ideally with others—precedes the visit, while discernment follows. The young person then has more than one option and does not make decisions for convenience's sake. Parents and friends would provide input and guide the young person in a good choice. The student understands and agrees with the site's stated mission. The environment is familial and the assigned tasks are neither overwhelming nor too simplistic.

An example of a perfect placement process would thus be as follows: The young volunteer would call and receive a warm welcome, securing an invitation to spend time in the agency as a guest before coming for an interview. The interview would include an informative tour of the facility, helping the young person to interpret what he or she observed. The interviewer would explicate the goals and objectives of the program, and the student would be able to understand the mission and work in a societal context. After the interview, the student could describe the population served, the staff configuration, and the role of potential volunteers. The young volunteer could easily translate the goals of the program into the universal principle of neighborly love and could also observe staff and volunteers caring for each other and the population they serve. The student would then be challenged into a decision-making process. The student volunteer would receive on-site training, support, and a regular opportunity for discussing progress and growth. Issues would be dealt with in a timely fashion and suited to the young person's development. The young person's sense of pride, growth, and love for those served would deepen with each visit.

> Young volunteers must be clear about whom they are serving, as well as the methods and mission of their service. They work best when they are confident and feel part of the team living the mission. They want to feel close to the people they serve.

While it may be mere dreaming to expect that sites be prepared to develop and support young volunteers to the degree just described, educators need to work collaboratively to provide the fundamentals of this scenario. Young volunteers must be clear about whom they are serving, as well as the methods and mission of their service. They work best when they are confident and feel part of the team living the mission; they want to feel close to the people they serve. Young people are ripe for being a part of something greater than themselves.

Adequate training, regularly scheduled assessment, and task variety are essential to ensuring the continued growth of a young volunteer. Simply being onsite does not enable young people to grasp the meaning of their work, and so the supervisory role must include an ongoing means of reflection. Theological reflection is the concrete goal for Catholic education. Young people often need reminders about the relationship of their work to a broader context and the spiritual meaning of the work.

A lack of new opportunity is a challenge that can be seen in programs that require an ongoing commitment. A student who is still copying and stapling after two years of service in a childcare center is probably not only bored, but has missed many opportunities for the grace, growth, and relationship that service ministry should offer. The reality that the childcare center has copying and stapling to be done each week cannot, even out of real necessity, prevail over the need of a young person to experience new situations and develop. Supervisors can be task-oriented to the extent that the focus on a volunteer's growth is missed completely. Repetitive, simplistic tasks with no one helping the young person see the value of their presence is at best counter-productive and at worst a deterrent to future service involvement by the adolescent. In defense of supervisors, most have added this task of working with students as an added responsibility to an already Herculean job description.

Selecting Sites for Projects vs. Programs

Obtaining adequate sites for single event service does not require the same fastidious concern needed for ongoing service programs. Projects require that a short-term need be met and that the student have a meaningful experience. However, the experience will lack meaning if the context is not clear or if students never encounter those for whom their contribution is meant. For example, a cleanup day for a newly purchased house at an AIDS center becomes a richer experience when young people work side-by-side with individuals who will live or work in the house. Jesus never separated Himself from the poor, the lame, and the lowly. As His disciples, Christians must never remain content with service that separates them from others' presence.

The preparation of students, whether for single event projects or for ongoing programs, needs a Gospel context, earnest reflection, and an understanding of the community need. Service must bring the young volunteers into direct contact with the population they serve. It must also be situated in such a way that the young person sees the whole picture and their individual contributions within it. This connection opens the door to effective evaluation of Gospel requests.

Generating enough satisfactory sites for ongoing service opportunities can be a great challenge. One obstacle to providing effective placements comes in the lack of sites willing to manage educational objectives. Since the explosion of service requirements, an increasing number of schools and parishes approach the same sites for student placement. The situation can be improved by using creative methods in finding different sites. Collaborating with other schools and programs can also be useful. Single sex schools often find it an advantage to partner with their brother or sister school for service. This provides young men and women the opportunity to connect not just socially but in the exercise of Gospel values.

> *The preparation of students, whether for single event projects or for ongoing programs, needs a Gospel context, an earnest reflection, and an understanding of the community need.*

Selecting Sites that Support Ministry

Catholic educators will need to engage sites that understand the nature of Catholic social teaching. As such, acquiring ample appropriate sites can be a challenge. It is important to be honest in regards to requirements when recommending sites to young people. If the selection process is weak, preparation and reflection will be compromised. Choosing sites appropriate to the intended educational outcome makes it possible for the site to support the goal of discipleship, rather than simply volunteer work. Each diocese should have a social justice committee and a charities funding program. These are good places to begin in seeking out agencies with a Gospel-directed mission. Another good idea is to host an afternoon or evening for site supervisors and young people to discuss mission and ministry. Young people should be involved in the planning of such events and should be provided with content from the social justice documents of the Church.

Generating Favorable Service Sites

The following are steps that should be taken in order to estab-lish favorable service sites for students.

1. ESTABLISH AN HISTORICAL PICTURE OF YOUR SCHOOL OR PARISH'S SERVICE.

Begin a search for sites by analyzing the nature of your school's service to others. A review of the situation might ask questions such as: "What have we done in the past?" "What are the tradi-tional projects or programs we are known for locally?" "Who is re-sponsible for carrying these out?" "What pictures, honors, and sto-ries still exist among the members of the community that highlight past service efforts?" If the student council or honor society spon-sors an annual service project, include this in the overall plan and thus eliminate the "recreation of the wheel" syndrome. Allow stu-dents who have been involved in other service experiences to share these with the group. Ask what made past events successful and help the community to replicate the success. Frequently, stories are carried from siblings who have shared their experiences at home. The collective history holds much that can regenerate former projects.

Possessing a good perception of past projects is helpful for fu-ture planning and allows educators to retain benefits already hap-pening. This is a good time to review service efforts in light of the school's mission. Perusing past and current efforts can better equip educators to make relevant service choices. This can involve look-ing through school yearbooks, past programs, and other service-relevent materials. Likewise, interviewing members of the entire community has the advantage of telling stories and helping as-sess the meaning of service to the community.

2. PERUSE THE CURRICULUM WITH AN EYE ON SERVICE AND CONSTRUCT PROGRAMS THAT SUPPORT LEARNING.

The curriculum offers intrinsic opportunities for creating ser-vice projects. Science classes protecting the environment, math-ematics classes responding to the Jubilee call for a reduction in debt of poorer countries, or social studies classes collaborating with local historical or preservation societies are a few examples of likely connections. There can also be value in service projects without a clear course connection. One such example is an annual Christ-mas toy collection sponsored by the faculty of the science department, with students in their respective science classes carrying it out. It is a powerful witness that the service role belongs to everyone. In addition, allowing students to view teachers in a ministerial role enhances the likelihood of developing discipleship within the entire school community.

3. DETERMINE SUITABILITY AND CONTACT POTENTIAL SITES DIRECTLY.

A simple phone call to the right person with a succinct conversation about service objectives can open the door to a new opportunity or easily eliminate a site from the prospect sheet. Timing is everything. Not all sites are in need at the same time, and not all are prepared at any given time to take on new volunteers. Therefore, do not fail to re-approach an agency even if years ago they did not need your participation. Be clear that not all sites will be able to meet the need of developing disciples, and never compromise this essential element. Remember that local Catholic Charities or Diocesan funded programs have a vested interest in helping educators to develop disciples.

4. CHECK WITH PARENTS TO LEARN ABOUT HELPFUL CONNECTIONS.

Many times I have found through casual conversation that the parent of a student is either a director or employee of a community service agency. Also, parents are usually supportive in placing students in service positions. The likelihood that a student wants to volunteer in an agency where his or her parent works or volunteers also exists. Encouraging students to work together with their parents has brought about very positive results. Such experiences allow for increased communication between parent and child, easy handling of transportation and scheduling issues, and a fostered admiration between both parties. It also happens that parents prove to be wonderful resources for training and preparing volunteers in particular fields. Strong parental participation enhances any service project or program.

5. HAVE STUDENTS LOOK THROUGH LOCAL NEWS STORIES TO DETERMINE NEEDS.

As my *Peace through Justice* course has proven time and time again, students are very good at determining community need. The local newspaper is one place to begin. Reading editorials or news stories that describe local tragedies can awaken students to community need. Once they have an idea, students are boundless in their energy to truly make a difference.

6. POLL FACULTY AND STAFF TO DETERMINE WHERE THE ADULT COMMUNITY PUTS ITS ENERGY.

Again, an effective use of networking is very helpful. One year we decided to honor the adults in our school community for their volunteer work. Consequently, a list of new service sites that students could approach was generated. Teachers and staff were delighted to introduce young people to the appropriate people at these service sites. Also, it was encouraging for the young people in our community to realize the number of adults who performed service on a regular basis.

7. COLLABORATE WITH OTHER SCHOOLS AND ORGANIZATIONS.

Demands on volunteer sites can be overwhelming, and most social service agencies are limited in time and available resources. Sites are more willing to accommodate when they receive fewer demands and even clearer expectations. Prior to teaching in a Catholic school, I worked in a low-income housing project, coordinating a family day care program for infants and toddlers from abusive and low-income families. I had a number of high-schoolers volunteer each day of the week. Having been on both sides of the court, I can say that the game gets played best when it is organized well. Students help both themselves and their volunteer sites when effective collaboration eliminates extra work. Working together also opens up the opportunity to share resources, ideas, struggles, and solutions.

8. INVITE LOCAL AGENCIES AND FAMILIES TO AN OPEN HOUSE.

On several occasions, my school has invited agencies and parents to come to the school and set up an information table. The response has always been positive. The service sites have an opportunity to recruit, and the parents have an opportunity to learn about service safety, agency requirements, transportation, hours, and other pertinent agency information. The setting can be much like a typical college fair with booths to display information.

9. ALLOW STUDENTS TO SHARE THE SERVICE IN WHICH THEIR FAMILIES HAVE BEEN INVOLVED.

There are an amazing number of families who do service together. I have learned that young people love to tell their family stories. The stories they tell include singular service experiences and ongoing family commitments. Using class storytime to generate ideas and discuss service sites helps to both name and respond to obstacles and strengths of various opportunities. Engaging other students in service experience critiques and assessing the strengths and weaknesses of sites helps prepare students for choosing and working with their own sites.

10. CONTACT ALUMNI OR ALUMNAE TO FIND HELPFUL CONNECTIONS.

Alumni are in a prime position to help find good sites. They already have a good understanding of the school's mission, programs, and projects. Having experienced these goals and objectives, they have a wonderful perspective on this part of the curriculum. They, like parents and faculty, also have connections. Some may even work in organizations where they could mentor a young student. The alumni newsletter or school's web page are excellent ways to enlist their help.

Generating sites is not always the great deal of work it seems to be. There are many strategies to help service coordinators find places where their students will have truly good experiences, where their contributions are valued, their growth and spirituality are nurtured, and they are prepared to go out to all the world as the disciples God calls them to be.

An Additional Word About Communication

It cannot be underscored enough that most of the problems associated with maintaining a strong service program are related to communication issues. Maintaining quality communication is time intensive and challenging for the average teacher. The need to solve problems early, the obligation to check in with both students and supervisors on a regular basis, and the amount of affirmation needed by most students usually takes more time than educators are allotted for service programs. Many schools do not have the luxury of a full-time staff person in the area of service; normally it is the religion teacher or campus minister who oversees the students' service requirements. While economics usually dictate this arrangement, it hampers effective communication. Teaching a full course load and trying to keep up with the communication needs of offsite service programming is next to impossible. Weakened communication usually leads to more serious problems, the very least being an unsatisfying ministerial experience for the student and

the worst being that service is reduced to simply one more require-
ment that students resent having to meet. In this case, less could
be more. It might be better to have fewer programs with good student experiences than to overwhelm everyone for the sake of com-
pleting numerous volunteer hours.

Working effectively with program practicalities is just as necessary for developing disciples as is the spiritual formation. With
challenges anticipated and solved early, the focus on prayer and
discipleship is more likely to remain first in everyone's awareness.

Chapter 6

Meeting Challenges as Jesus Did

Jesus' Paradigm for Meeting Challenges

The Gospels often portray Jesus at prayer. It is not unintentional that much of his prayer precedes ministerial action. Before beginning His active ministry, Jesus retreated to the desert for forty days of prayer and fasting. His greatest ministerial act, the work of the cross, began with the prayer in the Garden of Gethsemane. Jesus often retreated to quiet places, even taking a boat to get away from the crowds. These accounts show the most crucial distinction between ministry and volunteerism. Whether supervisor or volunteer, all must embrace service ministry with a deep prayer life.

Jesus' desert experience serves as a model for facing the challenges of Catholic service learning. The Gospels tell the story of Jesus' forty days in the desert, and each Gospel places it after Jesus' baptism, just prior to the beginning of his Gallilean ministry. With baptismal grace and a serious prayer life, Jesus faces the challenges of ministry.

Luke's Gospel (Luke 4:1-13) states that when Jesus was baptized, he was "full of the Spirit" and was led by the Spirit into the desert to be tempted. With the guidance of the Holy Spirit, He made the journey with wisdom, knowledge, counsel, understanding, holiness, and fortitude. Faced with evil personified, the famished Jesus was invited to fill his bodily hunger by turning stone into bread. This is a moment when Jesus certainly could have been forgiven for taking the easy way out. But He would have filled His most basic need the wrong way. God's Word reminded Jesus that "it is written that one does not live on bread alone," and thus, all people must depend on God alone.

Overcoming an obsession to fill one's own needs is a challenge in a success-driven culture. However, each person must overcome this drive so that he or she is empathetic enough to walk with those whose basic needs are not met. Jesus' success in momentarily giving up the thought of bread allowed Him to center on God. This is an important lesson for loving servanthood, one with which Adam and Eve were first to struggle. The idea of each person meeting his or her basic needs is important for working with the poor who often live in settings that can easily strip others of one of people's most fundamental needs, our personal security. Compromising one's security usually goes hand in hand with direct service to the poor.

Persisting, the Devil promised Jesus "all the glory and authorities of all the world kingdoms." People could accomplish a great deal in their ministry if they had all that glory and authority! But Jesus showed that it is necessary only to serve God. There is something inherent to authentic ministry that eliminates a desire for glory. This is counter-cultural in a society that feeds on self-affirmation. Jesus, however, preached that all people would be strengthened by facing the only challenge worth meeting—serving God.

The Spirit led Jesus to the desert, and the Spirit sustained Him in His trying moments. Luke begins the passage following Jesus' temptation thus: "Then Jesus, filled with *the power* of the Spirit, returned to Galilee...." Jesus went to pray and was filled with the power of the Spirit. Facing the challenges of service in a similar way, filled with the Holy Spirit and empowered by the Spirit, followers of Christ also send out their disciples to minister.

Having dealt with the temptations of turning stone to bread, with putting God to the test, and with false worship, Jesus was made ready to let the power of God work in Him. This alone prepares one for ministry. Educators need to design service experiences that pass the test of trust, that remain focused on God's work, and which are strongly rooted in Scripture and Catholic social teaching. It is as such that educators face the challenges of developing young disciples prepared to avoid these same temptations.

Prayer that precedes service is a centering time, an opportunity to encounter the Spirit who fortifies what people do. Luke reports that soon after reaching Galilee, Jesus was rejected. Undaunted, He went to His town synagogue to proclaim the Spirit's influence on His ministry: "The Spirit of the Lord is upon Me, for He has sent Me to bring glad tidings to the poor. He has sent Me to proclaim release to the captives and recovery of sight to the blind, to let the oppressed go free, to proclaim the year of the Lord's favor" (Luke 4:16-19). Graced with Baptism, prepared with the experience of prayer, Christians meet challenges, obstacles, and rejection as Jesus did—with the fullness of the Holy Spirit.

> *Educators need to design service experiences that pass the test of trust, that remain focused on God's work, and which are strongly rooted in Scripture and Catholic social teaching. It is as such that educators face the challenges of developing young disciples prepared to avoid these same temptations.*

Local, National, and Global Awareness

Another programmatic challenge is addressing the necessary balance of local, national, and international experiences. The option for the poor includes the neighborhood, the country, and the world. Eventually, all come to understand that there is a systemic connection among these. Effective programming with young people should include all three domains. The growing number of youth serving in their local cities and towns, as well as the growing number of national and international service experiences for young people, is a testament to God's call for them. The resources are present if educators accept the challenge of reaching out beyond their immediate surroundings.

This brings us to the subject of liability, a legitimate concern but not a brick wall for schools and parishes involved with direct service to the poor. Jesus told the rich young man to give up what he had and follow Him. Jesus approached the original twelve with the expectation that they were to simply follow. There is not any mention of Jesus even explaining the risks and liabilities to those He called. The element of trust is an expected essential for the follower of Jesus.

> The element of trust is an expected essential for the follower of Jesus. This is not to understate the need to consider the issues of liability; it is to suggest that these should not control ministry opportunities.

This is not to understate the need to consider the issues of liability; it is to suggest that these should not control ministry opportunities. At the very least, a formal, written agreement signed by the agency, student, parent, and a school representative will offer some protection. The school should also be aware of its insurance coverage for off-site situations regarding students. However, educators are reminded that they are called to take up their cross and follow Jesus, liability notwithstanding. All are commanded to be brother and sister to the poor and oppressed without personal safety as a condition.

The Challenge of the Spiritual and Corporal Works of Mercy

The spiritual and corporal works of mercy give clarity about what all people are called to do. Everyone can visit prisons and hospitals, get close to someone who is hungry or thirsty, or give away the many unused clothes in their closets. Any of these, however, can be a real challenge. Moving from a "comfort zone," all people are called to go to the physical and spiritual places where

Jesus hurts. There is not a lack of understanding about a preferential option for the poor; however, there is great fear that as people stand in solidarity with the poor, they will lose their own comforts—both physical and spiritual. And yet, a close proximity to the poor ones of the earth is precisely what the spiritual and corporal works of mercy ask.

Will giving a cup of water in the name of Jesus really bring people to heaven? Yes, because to do even one act purely for God has such a profound impact on the soul that it is eternal. It is not easy in the current milieu to give up home, family, and comforts. However, adults have not shown young people the real Jesus if they keep themselves physically distant from the oppressed. Trust and careful planning to avoid unnecessary hazards are needed. I am humbled by the trust of parents whose children have traveled with me to Haiti and Kenya. The response to this humility was to take very careful care of their children. These parents, though worried, were able to place their children in God's care. They were open to the Spirit calling their sons and daughters to meet God in the poor.

Developing Ministers

The most overwhelming challenge, the very subject of this book, is to foster ministry and to keep discipleship at the core of all that is done. So much is needed to develop a minister. The ability to move beyond the surface of things, such as paperwork and schedules, and into the heart of the matter, while sharing the Good News with God's beloved, is an incredible labor of love. Patience and endurance are needed in great measure.

Some helpful strategies in this area include:
- Constancy in assisting students to formulate competent connections to the Gospel.
- Maintaining the "two feet" approach: direct service and social change.
- Developing and maintaining a reflective process that considers personal and spiritual growth.
- Moving beyond "safe service" to the Gospel call to be with the poor.

These points bear the repetition found throughout this book, since they represent the core differences between the service practitioner and the disciple. These define Christian ministers.

Supervision

Another challenge to service learning is supervision. This challenge needs dual consideration, both at the site and at the school or parish. Extending the learning beyond the starting point requires shared supervision. This can be either an added complication or an added grace. Again, the importance of good site selection is key. A site that supports the intended outcome will be easier to work with. Thus, the best-case scenario is shared: an open and effective communication between the young person, the site, and the school or parish supervisors. Most programs handle this through paperwork, and while legalities do require some type of recording, sharing supervision should then move beyond paperwork. Phone or email notes, as well as occasional gatherings, keep relationships alive and nourished and are far better than a sheet signed by the site supervisor that a young person has fulfilled the time obligation.

Ongoing communication is time intensive; it includes visits to the site, phone calls, and participation in discussions that involve more than a few minutes call. The administration needs to support such time intensive work with adequate staffing. This is a challenge for many programs whose service coordinators double as teachers, campus ministers, parish religious education coordinators, and a host of other roles. Realizing that social justice education is at the core of Catholic education, educators should not hesitate to hire one or more full time people to facilitate this programming.

This segues into our next challenge: hanging in for the long haul. The commitment necessary from the administration, staff, young people, and sites must be strong enough to accept the wear and tear of long-term programs. Creating an effective and strong social justice education program, one that truly develops disciples, requires much time, energy, and work. Repetitive service can easily become ordinary and mundane. Keeping the program, the disciple, the leadership, and the sites alive and renewed is a challenge of the first order!

ESSENTIAL POINTS REQUIRING LONG-TERM ATTENTION

- Insuring that young people are developing new skills and growing spiritually.

- Seeing that the program and site supervisors are developing new skills and growing spiritually.
- Maintaining adequate communication with students, teachers, parents, and site supervisors.
- Detecting and healing ministry burnout.

IDEAS FOR GENERATING PROGRAM ENTHUSIASM

- Tell stories often—stories enliven the mission.
- Celebrate student and adult volunteers.
- Perform service with a school club, or with faculty, staff, students, and parents.

There are no miracle solutions to the challenges humans encounter, unless they accept the miracle of grace that comes through the Holy Spirit. It may seem simplistic and incomplete to some, but it seems that many people have cut short the process Jesus went through in the desert and have yet to try Jesus' model. If educators want to be true disciples who call their students to become true followers, they must labor continuously, never compromise the truth, and place their complete trust in the One whom they follow.

There is a great blessing to be received in meeting the challenges of ministry and discipleship. Undoubtedly, many who heard Jesus' beatitude sermon did not react with profound joy as they went home burdened with their immediate problems. The promise of eternal joy did not do much to put food on the table. However, food comes to the table as a result of trust, and this trust leads to a joy that can never die. Perhaps, since all obstacles have not been moved from view, all people are left wanting. This is truly a positive thing as the disciple now turns to God who is the true source of help for the challenge.

Chapter 7

Building a Civilization of Love: Service and the Next Generation

C ountless Christians have preceded us in effecting the reign of God and countless more will follow. To help initiate the next generation of Christian disciples, educators must approach service learning with precision, love, and humility. First and foremost, educators witness the call to love with their own lives. With skill, they assist young people in finding the particular grace God offers them, and in humility they rejoice with them as they engage in the personal call to discipleship.

Building a civilization of love is the duty of each Christian. This is accomplished by embracing the lifestyle of a disciple. Whether single, married, clergy, or religious, the common lifestyle is discipleship. Scripture and the Catholic tradition clearly define the hallmarks of discipleship. These are differentiated from the secular spirit of volunteerism. The vocation to build the reign of God, establishing a civilization of love, should be readily visible in the daily life of each Christian. Servanthood is only one aspect of living a full Christian life, albeit, one of the most important. The qualities of Christian service and discipleship include committing to a life of prayer, pursuing and accepting God's grace, living the Word, following God's ethics, and practicing communal responsibility. Service learning is an important way to help young people establish and grow in their Christian personality. There is no call quite like it. It is a humble honor to be invited by God to such an awesome responsibility.

Hallmarks of Authentic Discipleship

Marked with the sign of Baptism and with a growing awareness of faith, young people give service as true disciples when the following hallmarks are distinctive in their service to the Reign of God:

- Prayer is distinctive and interconnected with service.
- God's abundant grace is recognized.
- God is seen as the source of the good accomplished.
- In order to accomplish the miraculous, God sometimes asks the ridiculous.
- Disciple action is communal.
- Disciples measure by God's standards, not human standards.
- Disciples possess humility.
- Ministry is focused on the poor.

Prayer is Distinctive and Interconnected with Service

...Teach us to pray they said... and the master said...Abba, holy is Your name...Your kingdom come...on earth as it is in heaven...Give us today our daily bread...forgive our sins as we forgive those who sin against us...lead us not to the test, but deliver us from evil....

One can readily imagine the disciples' desire to pray as they had so frequently observed Jesus at prayer. Jesus was steadfast in His example to retreat to deserted places to commune with the Father. It was only natural that His eager, small band of followers wanted to do the same. The prayer He taught them, the Lord's Prayer, is very revealing both in its simplicity and its practicality. First, Jesus taught the disciples to turn to God with affection, informally approaching God as Abba, or "daddy." They were to eliminate and erase lofty and distant images of God. After venerating God and pursuing the arrival of the kingdom, the disciples were to pray for what they needed that day. Being well acquainted with human weakness, Jesus instructed them on the dual need to forgive and be forgiven. Finally, the prayer ends seeking strength in the midst of evil, a necessary request for those whom Jesus sends out like sheep among wolves.

The Lord's Prayer, probably more rightly described as "The Disciple's Prayer," offers some practical spiritual advice for young servant disciples. Each person should pray with great affection for God and reverence God with an expectation of building the world as he or she perceives heaven. One should pray for forgiveness and to be forgiven, for all people commonly hurt even when they are trying to help. All should then ask for what they need. Most importantly, one should count on the strength of God to face trials, knowing with certainty that He will help. The practicality of this prayer offers a good basis for the spiritual and temporal needs of young people performing Christian service. It can help them reflect on their basic and spiritual needs as they come to know the God of Love who calls them, establish new relationships, work for systemic change, and adopt a lifetime habit of bringing God's reign to reality.

While praying with a young African man from the Samburu tribe of Kenya, I noted that he ended his prayer not with "Amen," but rather with "And God said, all right." He then shared this custom with me. It illustrated his confident belief in God's confirming presence. Soon thereafter, it became my habit as well to conclude prayer this way, and it has had a powerful impact on my prayer life. It reflects a stronger belief that God is with me, eager to listen and answer my prayers. I am aware of the power of God blessing my prayerful efforts. God, the Alpha and the Omega, always has the last word. Many young people I know now also end prayer this way, and it has been very encouraging for them. Young people developing a prayer life need to experience God blessing their efforts.

Establishing the routine of a strong prayer life that is regular and gratifying is a challenge for all people, but especially for young people. Finding quality time for quiet reflection, securing sources that are relevant for their young prayer styles, and sustaining the discipline of regularity are real challenges for the youth of today. And yet, to approach service as discipleship, one simply must have a routine of nourishing prayer. A reflection on the simple tenets of the Lord's Prayer is a good beginning. Young people know the words, have familiarity with it in individual and communal settings, and can be led deeply into simple but profound ideas related to their service work. Moreover, the service experience itself can provide the desire to develop the practice of prayer. I have witnessed young people whose love for the elderly they visit each week or whose work with the children in Special Olympics so moved their hearts that they transitioned into regular prayer without even realizing they were developing discipline and habit. However it happens, the young disciple must acquire the habit of prayer relative to the service experience.

Recognize and relying on God's Abundant Grace

The Gospel recounts the apostles gathered around Jesus. The day was late, people were hungry and tired, the babies were cranky, and the mothers and fathers were worn out. They had been listening to Jesus for hours and had lost track of the time. Jesus commanded his disciples to feed the crowds. However, they were in the middle of nowhere, with no place to get food, and the late hour made travel impossible. Only able to gather a couple of loaves of bread and a few fish, the disciples probably looked at Jesus with fear or curiosity, amazement or trust, or maybe even disdain. But Jesus looked with compassion on the crowd, in empathy with the state of their hungry hearts and stomachs. He had the disciples organize the group into smaller groups, and He looked up to heaven with the small amount of food and prayed. He blessed and broke it, and when all had eaten, there was plenty left over. How did so little become so much? How was this abundance procured?

Jesus treated the situation as though very little of the material was needed, but rather a great deal of the spiritual. He turned heavenward in prayer, thus opening the door for a great abundance. The feeding of the multitude suggests that abundance comes from clearly knowing the need, organizing it, and then lifting oneself into God's presence to embrace the grace given.

There is an incredible power in accepting God's grace. The disciples did not recognize the power that was before them until the action of Jesus made it apparent. So it is with all people. The servant discipleship to which all are called requires openness to the miraculous made possible by recognizing the needs of those being served and presenting them to God. This is not a simplistic prayer for a miracle. Our belief and participation in God's abundance brings about all that is needed. Jesus models something quite essential about discipleship here. He shows that with very little resources, people can, with the grace of God, create an abundance to fill the needs of many. Modern scriptural scholarship speculates that Jesus' organizing of the crowd, followed by the blessing, breaking, and sharing bread, encouraged others to do the same and the sharing of what little each one had became an abundance for the crowd. If modern scholarship is correct, then Jesus' great lesson that day was his action—namely, service learning.

If I could give each young person I know a single gift, it would be the awareness that God is present always and everywhere. I wish for them to experience the maxim that hangs on the wall in my kitchen: "The will of God will never lead you, where the grace of God cannot keep you." The young have a supersensitive need to know that God is involved with their lives. The natural doubts and questioning of their youth can leave them fearful that they are moving further away from God. Paradoxically, it usually brings them closer.

> *People eventually come to know and trust that abundance is the result of accepting grace.*

People eventually come to know and trust that abundance is the result of accepting grace. Recognizing and working with the enduring presence of God comes from an arduous faith. Teaching young people to recognize grace as Mary Magdalene did at the Easter cave, or like Peter did in the dark on that stormy night of walking on water, is integral to helping them face the real limitations in the world that bring about the pain they might share in service experiences. Once they see with such eyes, they can rely on God's presence, trusting it to meet every situation.

God is the Source of the Goodness Disciples Accomplish

And does God not dress the birds like Solomon? And does God not know every single strand of hair on your head? And has not God given his very life for you? Has God not turned sinners to saints, and opened the eyes of the blind? Does God not give all people the very breath of their lives and sustain them each moment? Is the very heartbeat that gives life the result of God's providential care for you? Is this love that God has for each person not the source of every good thing they have ever done? For John's Gospel says, "God *is* love and who abides in love abides in God and God in them" (1 John 4:16). God is so extravagant with his children. Recognizing God's generous presence allows people to see what the good God accomplishes through them. Without God's love— the source of all life— people can do nothing. But as St. Paul noted, "I can do all things in Christ Jesus who strengthens me." Helping the young to recognize that God's Goodness is the source of Christian service allows them to use that Goodness more readily. It invites them to participate with God, it fosters the prayer and humility necessary for service work, and it teaches them the ways of God.

A regular reading of the Scriptures will keep the Christian service disciple in touch with the power of God operating in his or her daily life. Do not be afraid to introduce *lectio divina* to the young. The Psalms are particularly good for developing a realization that God is constantly working with us. *Psalms For Praying*, by Nan Merrill, is a very usable translation for young people. Also, using "thy will be done" as a mantra will help the young to let go and let God accomplish as they come to experience that all things work together for the good and glory of God. God's plan is undoubtedly far superior to any human plan, and yet, people often cannot see or understand it. The seasoned disciple trusts where good comes from and is willing to let God act as needed.

Disciples Follow in Humility

"Do not let your left hand know what your right hand is doing." "While in prayer go into your room in anonymity." "Be careful not to boast of your fasting with sackcloth and ashes." "Presume not on God, but trust in God's mercy" (Matthew 6:3, 5, 16).

Humility is a difficult virtue because, as Benjamin Franklin noted, proclaiming that one possesses it can serve only to prove that one does not have it at all. Franklin professed to have accomplished all the virtues but humility. People can end up feeling so good about what they do that they miss the point that God accomplishes it in them. It does not mean that they are not principle actors with God. They are, but far too often, people fail to acknowledge the actual source of the goodness they do.

> Humility is a difficult virtue because, as Benjamin Franklin noted, proclaiming that one possesses it can serve only to prove that one does not have it at all. ... People can end up feeling so good about what they do that they miss the point that God accomplishes it in them.

In moving from volunteer work to ministry, God is declared as the source of all good. Humility is not an intended outcome for secular programs, but it is a necessary one for Christian discipleship. Humility practiced well means that people have a proper view of God and themselves. They have neither boastful behavior, nor a lack of confidence. They follow, not moving ahead of God since everyone's proper place is under God's authority and care. People's position in the community should reflect that of a member of the mystical body of Christ. From the least to the greatest, each is fashioned in the image of God and should both respect others and themselves.

Humility is an important, but difficult virtue for the young to develop. For them, moving from the egocentric self to healthy confidence is a major developmental task. Service learning helps the young develop this virtue, as it repeatedly demands thinking and acting for others. People who work with adolescents see how easily they move from overconfidence to deep despair and back again. Both overconfidence and despair can be borne from poor self-esteem, a problem facing many young people. Humility is a virtue demanding maturity and a healthy self-esteem.

Community is Where Grace Abounds—The Disciple's Action is Communal

"Where two or three are gathered in my name, there I am" (Matthew 18:20). By the nature of Baptism, all people enter and live within God's communal activity. Formed by the action of the Holy

Spirit, a disciple's action is communal, as God is communal. The Church is communal; the fulfillment of the promise of Jesus takes place in the community. The Gospel of John presents a powerful scene of communal discipleship in its description of the Last Supper. Jesus and his disciples engage in community at its best as they pray, eat, and share stories, while they face one of the most difficult nights of their lives. It is within communal energy and grace that discipleship is conferred. The model of true servanthood takes place as Jesus bends down to wash the feet of His disciples, making it clear that disciple-servanthood is at the core of community. The disciple, unlike the volunteer, sees action and devotion in the communal command to serve as Jesus modeled the night before He died.

To Accomplish The Miraculous, God Sometimes Asks The Ridiculous

It is said that people must sometimes do the ridiculous in order for God to accomplish the miraculous. It is true. What shepherd would leaving 99 sheep to go find one? What Samaritan would take an injured Jew to an inn and pay all the expenses? Who would ever suggest that those who go to work at 5 AM and work until 5 PM should receive the same salary as those who begin at 9 AM or noon or 3 PM and work until 5 PM?

The disciple must come to grips with a life that is not a neat, perfectly wrapped gift to be opened with gentility and admired from the distance forever. Life is messy. It often does not make sense, and we must step out and take some risks that even our friends advise as foolish. Since there is no limit to God's love, and because God will go to any length to bring His people home, all people must go to the lengths modeled by Jesus. Jesus promised it would happen and told His followers to be happy "when they insult you and persecute you on account of Me" (Matthew 5:11). However, there is a difference between taking risks that guard personal care and safety and risking personal comforts. Far too often, people deem something ridiculous simply because it is inconvenient or because the loss of comfort frightens them. Finding a good balance between comfort and need is a necessity for the disciple. The disciple is called to go far beyond society's acceptable level of uncertainty. I do not promote putting the lives of others at physical risk, yet, it is evident that some risk is necessary in living out a preferential option for the poor. This is an area that needs careful thought on the part of administrators and staff.

Disciples Measure by God's Standards, not Human Standards

The parables are helpful in reminding people that God has a different set of standards. Jesus truly came to turn the apple cart upside down. Therefore, disciples know that it is not the numbers, the length of service, nor the order that counts. Disciples are confident that God's measure is deep within the soul, deep enough that even they cannot accurately measure themselves.

The world had strayed so far from God's measure that the Word became flesh, providing a firsthand experience of God's order. Consider for a moment the Magnificat. Soon after Mary realized that the Messiah was within her flesh, she clearly voiced the standard. It was a measurement that proclaimed a very different outlook than the Jews were expecting, "He has scattered the proud in the thoughts in their hearts; He has brought down the powerful from their thrones and lifted up the lowly; He has filled the hungry with good things, and sent the rich away empty" (Luke 1:51-53). When Jesus spoke for Himself, He repeated the same message in the Beatitudes, proclaiming the least likely to be the blessed ones. Who would have thought that the most blessed people would include the poor, the meek, the lowly, those mourning and weeping?

Today's young people are filled with dreams of being accepted into the best college and making their first million dollars by the age of forty. How do educators help them realize that the poor, the meek, and the lowly may be getting to heaven before them?

Utilizing these standards, Christians go about developing disciples whose service is complicated by the need to reject the world's view of success. This is especially difficult because young people are so attuned to the media's presentation of what is good, right, and necessary. Today's young people are filled with dreams of being accepted into the best college and making their first million dollars by the age of forty. How do educators help them realize that the poor, the meek, and the lowly may be getting to heaven before them? Service learning plays a critical role in bringing them into this view as they see the nearness of God in those they serve. It is difficult to break through the media messages that makes them cling to the security of worldly success, but educators must try.

The Poor are the Primary Focus of the Disciple's Ministry

The option for the poor has been singularly held in Christianity from the days Jesus walked the streets of Galilee until today. The volunteer can work anywhere, fulfilling the criteria for service, but the disciple eventually finds the way to a service that directly benefits the materially poor. This is the most unique of the hallmarks that separates discipleship service from volunteering. Also, it is the most challenging and shares a high priority with prayer. Christians simply are not disciples if they fail to reach out directly to the poor. It is the messiest part of the message, for people are not drawn to being scared, dirty, or fearful.

In the film *Entertaining Angels,* there is a powerful scene in which Dorothy Day enters a church and cries out loudly at Jesus on the crucifix saying, "I'm not who you think I am!" She chides Jesus, "You're dirty, and you smell, and you wet your pants and vomit." This powerful prayer shows a disciple face to face with ministry to the poor. Dorothy shows the frustrating side of working with the poor. For there is little romance in working with too few resources, too many problems, and all too few helpers. Despite its hardship and her hesitancy, Dorothy modeled that the true disciple servant remains with the ones Jesus is near.

Vision of the Reign of God

Consider the civilization of love. When people have made it to the Promised Land and when the objective is fully realized, what will it be like? What will the world be like when there is no need of disciples, volunteers, or service programs to heal wounds? What will it be like when all people are truly servants of each other? How will this civilization operate? Judy Chicago offers a great description in *The Dinner Party:*

And then all that has divided us will merge
and then compassion will be wedded to power
and then softness will come to a world that is harsh and unkind
and then both men and women will be gentle
and then both women and men will be strong
and then no person will be subject to another's will
and then all will be rich and free and varied
and then the greed of some will give way to the needs of many
and then all will share equally in the Earth's abundance
and then all will care for the sick and the weak and the old
and then all will nourish the young
and then all will cherish life's creatures
and then all will live in harmony with each other and the earth
and then everywhere will be called Eden once again.[25]

"AND GOD SAID, ALL RIGHT."

Endnotes

1. Jean Bertrand Aristide, *Eyes of the Heart* (Monroe, ME: Common Courage Press, 2000), p. 63.
2. Pope John Paul II, *XI World Youth Day Message*, November 1995.
3. Pope John Paul II, *XII World Youth Day Message*, August 1996.
4. Thomas Franklin O'Meara, OP, *Theology of Ministry* (New York: Paulist Press, 1983), p. 142.
5. Ibid, p 47.
6. Ibid, p. 47.
7. Hunger Project of the United Nations, http://www.fao.org.
8. CARE, http://www.care.org.
9. Institute for Food and Development, http://www.foodfirst.org.
10. National Catholic Conference of Bishops, *Sharing Catholic Social Teaching: Challenges and Directions: Reflections of the U.S. Catholic Bishops* (Washington D.C.: United States Catholic Conference,1998) p. 2.
11. Ibid, p. 11.
12. Pope John Paul II, *VIII World Youth Day Message,* August 1992.
13. _____. *VI World Youth Day Message,* August 1990.
14. _____. *VII World Youth Day Message,* November 1991.
15. _____. *VIII World Youth Day Message,* August 1992.
16. _____. *IX and X World Youth Day Message,* November 1993.

17.   _____. *XI World Youth Day Message,* November 1995.

18.   _____. *XII World Youth Day Message,* August 1996.

19.   _____. *Jubilee World Youth Day Message,* August 2000.

20.   _____. Closing Liturgy, *Jubilee World Youth Day,* August 2000.

21.   _____. Vigil of Prayer, *Jubilee World Youth Day,* August 2000.

22.   Ibid.

23.   _____. Closing Liturgy, *World Youth Day,* August 2000.

24.   The Alliance for Service Learning, *Standards of Quality for School-Based and Community-Based Service Learning* (http://www.quest.edu/slarticle.html).

25.   Judy Chicago, *The Dinner Party* (Viking Books, 1996).

Additional Resources

Books

Albom, Mitch. (1997). *Tuesdays with Morrie: An Old Man, A Young Man, and Life's Greatest Lesson.* New York: Doubleday. This is the true story about the love between a spiritual mentor and his pupil.

Brussat, Frederic and Mary Ann. (1996). *Spiritual Literacy.* New York: Simon and Schuster. An anthology of stories, quotes, and pearls of wisdom that has a significant section on service.

Gabriele, Edward F. (1995). *Act Justly, Love Tenderly, Walk Humbly.* Winona, MN: St. Mary's Press. A daily prayer book with a focus on peace and justice.

Gonzalez-Balado, Jose Luis. (1996). *Mother Teresa: In My Own Words.* New York: Gramercy Books. Anthology of Mother Teresa's prayers, quotes, and spirituality.

Harman, Willis. (1998). *Global Mind Change: The Promise of the 21st Century.* San Francisco: Berrett-Koehlers Publishers. This book brings into clear focus how unsustainable the modern way of life is. It also discusses the factors and forces that are already in motion to bring about global change.

Koch, Carl and Culligan, Michael. (1993). *Open Hearts, Helping Hands: Prayers by Lay Volunteers in Mission.* Winona, MN: St. Mary's Press. This book contains powerful prayers by lay volunteers in mission work.

Mattern, Evelyn. (1994). *Blessed Are You: The Beatitudes and our Survival.* Notre Dame, IN: Ave Maria Press. This text examines the eight beatitudes as attitudes necessary for peace and justice.

Puleo, Mev. (1994). *The Struggle is One: Voices and Visions of Liberation.* New York: State University of New York Press. The book includes reflections of life in base communities in contemporary Brazil. It informs and teaches liberation theology and vividly portrays Christian action in the community.

Rohr, Richard. (1991). *Simplicity: The Art of Living.* (Peter Heinegg, trans.) New York: Crossroad. The book presents the reader with the challenge to live in simplicity of mind, heart, and body — a call to revolution of the heart.

True, Michael. (1992). *To Construct Peace: Thirty More Justice Seekers, Peace Makers.* Mystic,CT: Twenty Third Publications. The book presents the portraits of 30 individuals devoted to non-violent social change.

Whitehead, Evelyn Eaton and James D. (1980). *Method in Ministry: Theological Reflection and Christian Ministry.* New York: Harper and Row Publishers. This book provides a method of practicing ministry that is inclusive of the community, your personal experience, and tradition rather than simply preaching to the reader.

Computer Web Sites

EDUCATIONAL METHODS AND SERVICE LEARNING:
RESEARCH, METHODS, ARTICLES
- http://www.quest.edu/summarysla.htm
- http://CSF.colorado.educ/sl/index2.htm

CATHOLIC RESOURCES:
CHURCH DOCUMENTS, HISTORIES, STATISTICS, AND NEWS ITEMS
- http://origin.org/ifv.cfm
- http://www.saintmarys.edu/~incandel/cst.html
- http://mindlink.net/fhooker/chdoc8.htm
- http://www.justpeace.org/docu.html
- http://www.catholicrelief.org
- http://www.vatican.va
- http://www.rc.net (Catholic News service)
- http://www.salt.claretianpubs.org/links.html
- http://www.coc.org (Center of Concern)
- http://www.cns.gov/learn/index.html
- http://www.cns.gov/learn/about/service/_learning.html (Service Learning)
- http://unicef.org

Bibliography

Freire, Paulo. *Pedagogy of the Oppressed*. New York: Seabury, 1974.

Groome, Thomas. *Educating for Life: A Spiritual Vision for Every Teacher and Parent*. CITY: Thomas More, 1998.

Merrill, Nan. *Psalms for Praying: An Invitation to Wholeness*. New York: Continuum Publishing Group, 1997.

NCCB. *Sharing Catholic Social Teaching: Challenges and Directions: Reflections of the U.S. Catholic Bishops* (Washington, DC: United States Catholic Conference, 1998.

The New American Bible. (Wichita: Fireside Bible Publishers,) 1996-97 edition.

O'Meara, Thomas Frankin, O.P. *Theology of Ministry*. New York: Ramsey Press, 1983 (First Edition).

Pope John Paul II. *The Gospel of Life*. New York: Random House, 1995.

Pope John Paul II World Youth Days 1990-2000.

WEBSITES:
- http://www.action.org
- http://www.care.org
- http://www.fao.org
- http://www.foodfirst.org
- http://www.quest.edu/slarticle.html
- http://www.unicef.org/sowc99/sw99rite.html

About the Author

For three decades, Pamela J. Reidy's youth ministry and service learning experiences have touched many lives. Beginning in 1971 and extending until 1984, she was the Director of Religious Education for four parishes within the Diocese of Worcester, Massachusetts. During that time, she served as a confirmation program coordinator, retreat director, liturgy chairperson, and parish folk group leader. Her ministerial talents subsequently led her to coordinate a family day care program and assist at an adolescent mental health care facility.

For the past sixteen years, Ms. Reidy has worked as a teacher and department chair for religious studies and community service learning at Notre Dame Academy in Worcester. She has held board membership on several associations, notably the Notre Dame Missions Volunteers; the Family Daycare Health Improvement Project; the Friendly House Multi-Service Neighborhood Center; and the Social Justice, Peace & Integrity of Creation Commission for the Diocese of Worcester.

Along with mentoring her students in the area of service learning, Ms. Reidy herself has volunteered at several social service agencies, including Hospice, CASA, and a local rape crisis center. Her experience with mission work has taken her to countries such as Haiti and Kenya on several occasions. A skilled lecturer, she has presented on numerous topics, including mission trips to Haiti, sexual abuse, and community service programs.